CW00537182

LD 4099303 5

Commercial Writing

Commercial Writing

How to Earn a Living as a Business Writer

Antonia Chitty

ROBERT HALE · LONDON

© Antonia Chitty 2009
First published in Great Britain 2009

ISBN 978-0-7090-8594-2

Robert Hale Limited
Clerkenwell House
Clerkenwell Green
London EC1R 0HT

www.halebooks.com

A catalogue record for this book is available from the British Library

2 4 6 8 10 9 7 5 3 1

Typeset in 9¾/12¾pt Palatino
by Derek Doyle & Associates, Shaw Heath
Printed in Great Britain by the MPG Books Group, Bodmin and King's Lynn

Contents

Introduction

Do you dream of earning your living from writing? Many people do, but few succeed. This book is full of authoritative expert advice based on practical experience, and will show you how to make writing a commercial business.

Read on if you:

- want to work for yourself on a freelance basis;
- might want to set up your own business;
- are interested in finding out how to develop skills for copywriting, marketing, press releases and more;
- would consider providing a service for businesses;
- want to be able to pay your bills every month;
- wish to restructure your life and make the move from employment to writing full time;
- and most importantly, perhaps, if you relish the idea of earning a living from writing.

Many people want to write, yet are unclear about how to make it pay. If you have had enough of trying to write in your spare time, and want to make the move to writing full time, this book will show you how. Commercial writing is a great way to use and develop your writing skills and earn a living. From the basics of getting started, different areas to specialize in, to finding and keeping clients, this book take you step by step through the process of becoming a professional writer.

Media life coach Joanne Mallon coaches want-to-be writers and those looking to change careers. She says:

> The urge to write doesn't go away. If you have a suppressed calling in your life it just calls out louder. I worked with a receptionist to help her find time in her lunch hour to sit in an unused office and write. Follow your dream; being a writer comes from within and won't go away. It is even better if you can take that dream and marry that to a job that pays the bills.

The first part of this book tells you what you need to get started. Read it to find out the equipment you will need. Find out about how to develop your skills and get useful training, how to set up a business and find clients. Each chapter includes tips from experienced writers on what works for them. There are recommendations of professional organizations to join to help boost your career and ensure clients trust your qualifications.

Through interviews and case studies, this book lets you into the secrets of successful business writers. You can learn from other writers' thought processes, decisions, successes and mistakes. In the second part, simple 'how to' guides take the mystery out of what you need to do to get started in different specialist areas:

- Advertising
- Corporate communications
- Marketing
- PR
- Journalism
- New media copywriting
- Speechwriting.

What this book will not do

This is not a guide for aspiring novelists. There are many other books that focus on those avenues. Try the *Writers' and Artists'*

Yearbook, an annual publication, which can help you find out about getting a publisher if you want to write books. Visit the website www.writersandartists.co.uk for a taste of what the book can offer. *The Writer's Handbook* is another guide to getting published. Both books are packed with contacts in the media world, accompanied by advice from successful authors. A&C Black, the publishers of the *Writers' and Artists' Yearbook* also offer the *Poetry Writers' Yearbook* and the *Children's Writers' and Artists' Yearbook*.

For journalists and authors

You will find essential tips in this book if you are an author who wants to make some extra income using your writing skills or a journalist looking to break into lucrative business writing. This book will help you if you are already writing for a living, but looking, as many journalists and authors do, for practical ways to increase your earnings. This book will help you diversify, find clients and develop a range of steady income streams to help balance out more precarious income sources.

Get writing

Whatever you want to do, the important thing is to make a start. Put pen to paper and plan out your writing career. Have a vision of where you would like to be in a year, and in five years. Then start putting some of the stages in place to help you reach your goals. Media life coach Joanne Mallon says:

> If you want to be a writer, then write. Whether it's a blog, a private journal or something for the local paper, it's important to keep developing your writing skills. Get used to letting others see your work and listening to feedback on it. Writing can be a very personal thing to do, but as a professional writer you will have to produce what your client or reader wants and adjust your work when necessary.

Read the different sections of the book, identify where you need practice, and sign up for a course if you think that will help. Joanne adds:

> Any career change will involve an investment of time and probably money, so think about what you need to do to make your move. Will you need to retrain, or to save enough to fund you for the first few months? What regular time/funds will you set aside to advance your writing career?

Start making your plans, read the useful information in this book, and you will soon find yourself on the route to a career as a professional writer.

PART ONE

How to do it

This section of the book looks at what you need to get started, skills, training, and how to set up a business and find clients. Read advice from experienced writers on what works for them, and discover the professional organizations that can help you.

Chapter 1

Getting started

If you already view your writing as a profession, and go about it in a business-like manner, you may just want to skim through this chapter. You will find plenty of tips for streamlining your working practices and making your business more efficient. If you currently are writing part time or as a hobby, read on for practical advice for getting your commercial writing career off to a good start.

Advice in this chapter may seem to be common sense, but by following it you can avoid costly mistakes, and ensure that clients view your business as professional and credible from day one. Do not skimp on important matters such as setting up your workspace correctly. A little time and thought at an early stage can save you from an aching back or repetitive strain injury.

Get writing

Perhaps the first and most important thing is to have some ideas about what you want to do. Do you see yourself in journalism, or would you like a career in public relations (PR) or copywriting? Start finding out about your options. Media life coach Joanne Mallon says:

> To change career completely, sometimes you have to take a sideways step first. So say you're an accountant but you want to be a magazine writer. A sideways step into that would be to look for an

accountancy job within magazine publishing. Then you're in a better position to look for opportunities to move from accountancy into writing. Either that or look for opportunities to move into a new writing job in your current industry, or use your current job to gain more writing experience – maybe write something for the company newsletter. If there isn't a newsletter, could you volunteer to start one? This could give you experience to offer your newsletter writing skills to other companies.

Where to work

When starting your own commercial writing business, you have a number of choices of where to work. You may want to work from home, rent a desk in a shared office space or lease business premises. The decision will be informed by the type of business you want to set up, and your reasons for doing it. If you simply want to work as a freelance copywriter in advertising, you may be looking largely for jobs based in client offices. If you have been motivated to work for yourself by the conflict between a full-time office job and the needs of a young family, a home office may be best. Where you live will also shape your decision: a large home with a dedicated study or even space for an office in the grounds may be a great place to start your business. A shared property with people coming and going at all hours may make it hard to concentrate, and be totally unsuitable if you have to meet clients.

Working from home
Many businesses start in the home. Unless you need a retail front this can be an excellent place to begin. You are minimizing your risk and start-up costs. You will save by avoiding office rental costs, and can take advantage of the fact that many homes now already have high-speed internet links and computer equipment. It is possible to offset some of your home expenses, such as utility bills, against your tax bill, based on the proportion of your home that you use for business. Check your own circumstances with your accountant or the Inland Revenue.

Writing from home works well if you live by yourself, or the rest of the occupants are out at work or school. Few writers can work efficiently in the midst of family hustle and bustle, and you will need some quiet space and time for important phone calls. Working from the kitchen table can put a limit on your 'office hours', as you will need to clear up for meals, so find yourself a separate desk space, even if it is only in a corner of another room.

Running a business from home can create some difficulties. You will be taking over a part of the home for work. Think about how this space was used before, and what you will do now. It can be simple to set up business in a little-used dining room, until you are asked to shift out for a big family meal. Also, think about how you will set the boundary between work and home life. If a client calls after you have finished work for the day, will you answer the call? A simple enquiry may take minutes out of your evening, or you could end up starting your computer, opening files and taking down detailed comments while your dinner burns. Mentally, it can be hard to walk away from a home-based business, and many writers find themselves working into the night.

Check with your local council and home insurance providers before you launch a home-based business. Find out what you need to do in the following areas:

- *Your local authority* Most authorities are reasonable: a computer and telephone-based writing business is unlikely to cause the same disruption as an import business with large lorries pulling up in front of a domestic property in a small street.
- *Business rates* You should also find out whether the part of your home used for business is liable for business tax rates. This is less likely if it is just you and a computer, but more so if you will have employees and clients on site, with part of your property exclusively for business use. Ask your accountant or the Inland Revenue for advice based on your circumstances.
- *House insurance* Insurers will be concerned if you intend to have staff or clients located at your property – this will not be

15

covered by a regular home insurance policy. Combined 'work from home' policies are available.

- *Equipment insurance* Check the level of cover for your office equipment too, and whether this will be covered by your home contents insurance. If equipment is used for both home use and work use, it may be covered, but if you start getting equipment solely for business use you need to think about business insurance cover. Check with your own insurance provider.
- *Your landlord* If you rent your property, you also need to read the terms of your lease to see if you are allowed to carry on a business from home. If this is excluded, it may be possible to negotiate a change in terms with your landlord.

From home, but not in the home
If you have enough space, a garden office could be a solution to keeping home and business separate without a long commute. If you are lucky, you may be able to convert an outbuilding. If not, there are a number of companies that will erect a small building in your garden. Many of these buildings come largely pre-built. You will need to think in terms of several thousand pounds for something that is secure and sufficiently well insulated for an office space. Ask your local authority planning department whether you will need planning permission too: this will depend on where you live, whether there are any covenants on the land, how close the building would be to neighbouring properties and other factors.

There are pros and cons to a garden office. On the plus side, you will be creating more space, and have an office to shut the door on at the end of the day, making a break between work and home. You are close enough to the house to nip home for a lunch break, without the temptation of the TV all day. If the family is being noisy, you can escape. On the downside, you will have the extra costs of installing the building and joining up supplies for heat and light. However well made, a stand-alone office will feel cold when you come in, so you will find your heating bills go up. Think carefully about security too: can you install an intruder light or alarm, so you don't come down to the office and find someone has broken in overnight and taken off with your computer equipment? Again, check with your insurance company whether equipment in a garden office is covered.

Working from home and clients

When you set up a business, you need to ask yourself how working from home will appear to clients. Partly, this will depend on the sector you work in. If you are dealing with multinational companies, staff may be less open to dealing with a home-based business than, say, if you are working mainly with other home-based and small businesses. This is not set in stone. If you have had a glittering career with your former company and are leaving to go freelance, they will be contracting with you for your skills, and less concerned about your location. If you have an excellent reputation, clients will seek you out, wherever you are based. And of course, if you take advantage of some of the technology touched on already in this chapter, and can prevent your kids answering your business line, clients may never need to know your exact office set-up. This works until, of course, you need to meet a client face to face.

Where to meet clients

Much of your writing business can be carried out over the phone and by email. However, there will always be occasions when it is beneficial to meet a client face to face. Do not panic if your home office is disappearing under piles of paper, the kitchen is full of dirty dishes, and you have to meet a client. There are plenty of other options.

First of all, start with the simple solution. Suggest you meet at their offices. If that is not possible, is there a suitable meeting place halfway between your home and the client's location? Long-term home workers become skilled at assessing venues for meetings. A coffee shop or bar is possible for a friendly informal meeting, but may not give the right professional impression for a new or important client. Check out the facilities at smart hotels in the right area. They may have a quiet coffee lounge or public meeting area with the required classy appearance to impress. Do some homework. Visit at the time of day you are likely to be meeting a client.

Confidently order a cup of tea, and sit down and observe whether other people are having meetings there. If you find a good location it can be invaluable.

You may want to become a member of a club. This will give you access to a smart meeting place in the centre of town. Membership of an organization for writers may get you a discounted club membership. For example, members of the Society of Authors can join the New Cavendish Club; London Press Club members get a discount at the Commonwealth Club. And some professional organizations have attractive offices with facilities for members, such as the Chartered Institute of Public Relations premises on St James's Square. Although the majority of UK clubs are in London, there are also a number in cities like Manchester, Edinburgh and Glasgow, Cheltenham and Chester.

When not to work from home
Working from home gives you plenty of flexibility. It can be nice to have a decent meal at lunchtime, cooked in your own kitchen, or sit on the sofa when you want a coffee break. However, do you have the discipline to switch the TV off when you really should be getting on with work? If not, a rented desk space or office may be a better option. While working from home is a low-cost way to get started, consider whether this will suit your personality. If you thrive on chatting round the water cooler, you may be better looking for freelance work at the client's premises or finding shared office space.

Working from client premises
Many freelance business writers spend much of their time working from client premises, which can avoid the need for anything but a basic office set-up at home. Working this way can feel much like having an office job but without the benefits like holiday and sick pay. It is harder to set your own hours, and you may feel it best to dress like others in the office. On the plus side you get to use the employer's facilities in the course of carrying out your work, and have colleagues on hand to consult, which can speed things up. Working in-house also keeps your profile high and can help you

network and get more work in a way that requires less effort than when working from home.

Shared office space

Setting up on your own can be daunting, and at the start of your career as a business writer you may not want to sign up for a long office lease, and the financial commitment that goes with it. There are several ways round this. In many towns there are now shared office spaces designed for small businesses and freelancers. Depending on the set-up, you may simply get a desk, but often you have access to meeting-rooms and the option for a phone line, telephone answering and broadband. Fees vary enormously: some office spaces are run by large commercial companies, while others are set up by development or enterprise agencies to help business growth. Some businesses with office space to spare may rent out a portion, or a few freelancers may get together to rent an office between them.

There are websites to help you find a desk space, including www.officesharing.co.uk, www.sparedesk.com and www.share-myspace.co.uk. Ask at your local enterprise agency or chamber of commerce. If you belong to a business network, mention that you are looking for space there too. (See Chapter 4 for more about networking.)

Once you have found a space, read the contract carefully. Here are some points to think about:

- How long is the contract for: can you give notice after a month or do you sign up for six months or a year? When is the rent reviewed?
- What does the basic fee include? How much extra do you need to pay for internet access and a phone line?
- Some shared office providers charge different amounts for a full- or part-time desk.
- Check when you can get access to your desk – it would be frustrating if you find the building closes at eight when you are still working to meet a deadline.
- What security is there? Remember that there will be a

number of other businesses in your building. Do you have lockable storage for all your work?

- Check out facilities for tea and coffee, meeting and break space, and ask about how often the office is cleaned.
- What other charged services are available? Will you have access to a fax or photocopier?

Renting a desk can be a great way to have a formal work space without a long-term financial commitment or expensive start-up costs. You will acquire a range of colleagues, which is great if you get lonely working on your own, but can be infuriating if someone is talking loudly on the phone while you want quiet to work. Weigh up the pros and cons, and visit the space a couple of times during the hours you would be working to check out who is around.

Setting up your own business premises

You may have a clear plan for how your commercial writing business will grow. If you are setting up a PR, advertising or marketing business you may see a future where you have a number of people working for you. This makes it more important to start thinking about proper business premises. There are a number of factors to weigh up.

Will you buy or rent a property? For many people, this is constrained by budgets. Renting is more flexible, and you have less responsibility, plus there is a smaller up-front investment. Remember that, on top of the rent, you will need to budget for:

- business rates
- utilities
- business insurance
- ongoing maintenance
- legal costs
- three or six months' deposit
- stamp duty (payable on all commercial leases).

When making your decision, you will also want to look at possible locations for your business. While a commercial copywriting business is unlikely to depend on passing trade, an office must be accessible for clients. Some parts of town will be more attractive than others to a media business. Think about how many desks you want to house. If you are starting small, will you move premises once you expand, or do you want somewhere with room for growth? If you are renting, how long do you want to tie yourself to a lease for? Check how often the rent is reviewed too. Will you need to make any alterations to the property, and will the landlord give you permission for this? Will you need planning permission too? Find out about building, fire and health and safety regulations, so you can check if your potential premises will comply.

Legal advice
Whether you decide to buy your own premises or rent an office, you should get legal advice on the contract. You may wish to consult a solicitor if you are signing up to a desk space too.

Lifestyle

Writing for a living can seem like a great lifestyle choice. Get up when it suits you, lounge around in whatever you want to wear, and have tea breaks whenever you want. If you speak to people who write for a living, you will find that it rarely works like that. If you need to meet deadlines, you can find yourself working from early morning to late at night, and eating lunch at your computer. If you need to meet clients, you may feel the need to dress to impress, yet find your wardrobe bereft of smart office clothes.

Be realistic when you are starting out. Decide on the hours you will work. Think of ways to give yourself a start and finish time, and try to stick to them as much as is realistically possible. If you are working from home it can become even more important to have a start and end to the day.

If you have children and run them to school, make a start when you get back. Their return from school may make a natural break in your day, or make it hard to work between three and seven. Many working parents find that they need to get back to their desk once their children are in bed.

If you are more in command of your own time, you may find it suits you to be very flexible. Some people do get the most work done when a deadline is approaching, and get a buzz out of cramming a weeks' work into a couple of days. Only you can tell whether you thrive on this sort of irregular working pattern, or if you will feel better knowing that you close your computer at 5 p.m. every day.

Deadlines and personal commitments

It can be easy, if you are writing to earn your living, to let writing take over your life to the detriment of relationships and your social life. As well as planning when you will get the work done, you may need to plan in your relaxation time.

In any freelance career, or when you run your own business, there is always the fear that the work will dry up, that you won't be able to pay your mortgage or meet other business bills. This fear can drive you to accept pieces of work when you don't really have time, or leave you working late into the night, long after you might have finished work if you were still an employee. Acknowledge this fear, and do what you can to keep your life in balance. There is nothing wrong with explaining to clients that you are currently fully booked, but could fit the work in at a named point in the future. While many clients want things done as soon as possible, most realize that you have other demands on your time. This can also make them value your work more, and book your time further in advance on future occasions.

There is more on finding and managing clients in Chapter 4. First, though, let's look at your office and what you need to run a successful commercial writing business.

Setting up your office

You can start out as a business writer without investing an enormous amount of money. You probably already have a desk and chair, a telephone, a computer, a printer and internet access. The important thing is to assess whether a set-up that has been adequate for a little writing in your spare time will still be comfortable if you are working all day, every day.

Healthy freelance working

When you are employed, there will be someone in the company responsible for your health and safety, and that includes ensuring that your seating, desk and computer position are not going to cause you problems in the future. When you are self-employed, the main person who will look after this is you. You may be able to get help in creating the right set-up for you to work if you are doing a prolonged stint as a freelance at one location, but this is unlikely if you are doing the odd day for a range of companies. Be clear on how you need to set up your workspace to be comfortable for the whole day, and adjust things as much as you can when you arrive at a new workplace.

If you are working from home or in your own office or rented desk space, you have the chance to get things just right for you. You should choose a desk that is the right height: an adjustable chair can help you get the desk at approximately elbow height when you are sitting up straight. This does not have to prove costly. You can make simple adjustments to the height of your chair with a cushion, and raise your computer screen on a couple of telephone directories.

Chairs

A good chair can be a great investment if you are working for yourself. Look for something with adjustable height, back and arms ideally, then you can adjust it to suit your height.

Tips for avoiding repetitive stress injury (RSI):

- Get your work station set up to suit you.
- Have your monitor, keyboard and mouse all within easy reach.
- Make sure your head, neck and shoulders are straight when looking at your work.
- Your upper arms should be by your side, not stretched forward.
- Keep your wrists straight and roughly parallel rather than bent in.
- You may be better off without the props at the back of the keyboard which can make your wrists bend upwards.
- Sit up straight instead of slouching: you may need to raise your screen.
- Ask for an assessment if you have an employer.
- Take short breaks regularly.
- Flex and stretch your arms, shoulders and neck at least once an hour.
- Visit RSI Action, www.rsiaction.org.uk, or contact RSI Awareness, www.rsi.org.uk, tel. 023 8029 4500 for more information.

Telephones

How much will you need to use your telephone as a commercial writer? Although you may envisage yourself sitting quietly typing away at your desk, making telephone calls is an essential part of your business and, as such, getting the right phone can help. See Chapter 2 for tips on how to improve your skills on the phone. In this chapter we will take a quick look at your choice of phone lines and equipment.

Do you need a business line?
If you work from home, assuming you choose broadband to link to the internet, it is possible to have only one telephone line for work and home. This can help keep your costs down when you are start-

ing out. There are a number of possible problems with having only one line, especially if you work out of the family home. It can be hard to stop children picking up important business calls, or teenagers from hogging the telephone line when you need to work. In the evenings, you may have mentally switched off and only be expecting calls from friends and family, but this doesn't stop clients calling. If you only have one line it makes it harder to leave work behind.

Mobile working

You may, instead, decide to run your business from your mobile phone. This will ensure that clients can get hold of you, and will avoid problems if you have to be out of the office. However, a business may appear more established and professional if it has a local phone number as well as mobile contacts. You also need to assess the quality of your mobile reception from your main workplace. There is nothing more frustrating than trying to interview someone or liaise with an important client when you can only hear half of what they say. Clients will soon get irritated too.

Running a second line

There are advantages to having a line specifically for your business, and in some situations it is obviously essential. If you have premises or rent an office or even desk space you are likely to need a business line. If you use a dial-up internet connection, consider getting a second line as otherwise existing and potential clients can find your phone line is engaged while you are online, which can put them off. You may be better investing the money you would have spent on a second line on getting broadband, which can speed up internet research and online communications.

Getting a good deal

There is no need to pay over the odds for your phone line. Shop around through websites such as www.u-switch.com that will provide a number of quotes. Look at your overall usage. Do you want a package that combines a mobile phone and a landline? You may want to include broadband too. As well as cost, ask around to check the sort of service people have received from phone providers that you are considering. It can be annoying to have problems with your home phone: when your business and income rely on reliable telephone and internet services your choice of provider is even more crucial. U-Switch offers customer reviews alongside the recommendations it makes for your particular needs.

If you are working from home, you may find that you do not need to go for a specific business package. As a sole trader or free-lancer these can be more expensive than other deals on offer.

Non-geographic numbers

You can purchase an 0845 number and direct it to your existing landline or mobile, or rent an 0845 line from a phone provider like BT. The advantage of this sort of number is that all customers will pay the same when they call you, regardless of their location and yours. You can also transfer the number if you move locations, which can be good if you are starting by working from home, but plan to move to an office in the future. It also means you have an alternative to giving out your personal or home number.

There are some downsides to offering a non-geographic number. Some people find them irritating, and worry that they will be paying over the odds for their call. Some phone providers offer discounts to numbers beginning 01 or 02, which do not apply to numbers starting with 08; these numbers are also rarely included in free minutes packages.

Different sorts of numbers:

- Numbers beginning 0845 are nominally local rate. Numbers beginning 0870 are charged at national rate. However, many providers exclude these numbers from discount packages, so they may end up costing your customers more.
- 0871 and 0844 numbers are charged at a rate fixed by the operator, subject to an upper limit, and are used by some companies to earn money.
- 0300, 0303 and 0306 can be used by public services and non-

profit organizations, such as charities; 0330 and 0333 are for any organization or individual, while 034x and 037x numbers will be available to other users currently using the equivalent 084x or 087x numbers. Calls to 03 numbers will cost no more than calls to standard geographic numbers, are not to be used to generate profit and will be included as part of inclusive call minutes or discount schemes.

VoIP

Voice over Internet Protocol (VoIP) is a way of using software on your computer to have conversations using the internet. There can be big cost savings. You do not have to have a geographic number, or can choose, say, a London-based number even if you are elsewhere. Calls may be free to other VoIP users on the same network, or can be charged by the minute. There may also be a flat rate connection fee and monthly subscription charges for some options. You can have your own telephone number, or people can contact you via a user name.

VoIP is an easy way to add an extra phone line to your home if you have a broadband connection. It can offer similar facilities to a regular landline: conference calls, call forwarding, automatic redial, for example. On the downside, call quality can be poor or variable, especially if you are part of a busy network. Reliability and quality are improving all the time. VoIP is not the solution if you send a lot of faxes: a landline will work better for this. VoIP calls are not usually encrypted at this time, which can make it easier for a determined eavesdropper. Examples of providers of VoIP include Skype, Googletalk, Windows Live Messenger and Yahoo Messenger. You will need a microphone and speakers attached to your computer to use VoIP.

Skype

Skype, one of the biggest VoIP providers, allows you to make and receive phone calls via your computer. SkypeOut lets you call local, international and mobile telephones, for a fee. SkypeIn lets you receive calls on your computers dialled by regular phone subscribers to a local Skype phone number. Skype-to-Skype calls are free. You can pay a small monthly fee for flat rate UK landline calls, a discount on a personal online number and voicemail. Alternatively, you can work on a pay-as-you-go basis, and upload money to use paid services. As a subscriber, you can create a number in any local area, and callers will pay the local rate to call that number. This can be an advantage if you want to appear to be UK based, while actually working from Spain, for example.

Computers

Mac or PC?
One of the fundamental decisions in choosing a computer is whether to go for a PC, a personal computer which is IBM compatible with Microsoft Windows as its operating system, or a Mac, a personal computer using the Mac OS (operating system). Traditionally, the world was split, with designers and graphic artists opting for Macs while almost everyone else used a PC. Taking this view can mean that you miss out on some good features available with a Mac, which can make it easier for anyone to manipulate images, music and video. On the other hand, with a Mac you are more reliant on Mac software, whereas with a PC there is a wider range of software from other companies. As Mac software is specifically designed for the Mac OS it does give a good performance, and is set up so you can get your Mac out of its box and start using it without lengthy installations. A Mac will only be compatible with Mac devices and peripherals. With a PC, you can end up with more minor irritations as you clog up your system with more and more extra peripherals and minor software errors. This can lead to slow running. Finally, Macs tend to cost more than PCs, both as an initial purchase and to fix if there is a problem.

As a business writer, you should also consider the system that your clients are using. It is possible to transfer work from a Mac to a PC and vice versa, but simpler to work on the same system. If you work with design-based businesses you will find Macs are popular, but more clients will have a PC. However, with practice you will be able to transfer documents with minimal problems most of the time.

This small section of this book is not the place to try to convert anyone from one type of computer to another. If you have been using a computer for a number of years, you are probably keen to stick with the operating system that suits you, and that you are familiar with. If you are making a new purchase, look at both Macs and PCs with an open mind. Try to find a store that will let you try out a system before you buy it.

Laptop versus desktop
Few freelance business writers start with a large enough budget to buy more than one computer. This means that you will proba-bly be choosing between a desktop model and a laptop. You will need to weigh up the possibly greater comfort of a desktop model with the portability of a laptop. Which one suits you best will very much depend on where you plan to work. If your work will take place in a range of locations, then a laptop is your best option. A desktop can be more affordable and it is easier to replace and upgrade parts of the system or increase the memory capacity.

Over time you may want to aim to purchase a second machine to use in case of problems with the first (see 'Back ups', page 37). Having a desktop for use in your office and a laptop to take to client meetings can be ideal, especially if you have a wireless network and can link the two machines back at your (home) office.

Internet access
A good internet connection can make the life of a commercial writer much easier. Big businesses will expect you to be able to receive files over the net: if you are a copywriter of any sort you may frequently be sent pdfs or image-heavy documents to check. If you choose to work in PR you could end up sending hundreds of emails each day. In either situation, a broadband connection will beat a dial-up one hands down, and makes it possible for you to

view video clips and music more easily too.

One difference between broadband and dial-up is that broadband is always on. What is more, you can access the internet and your emails at any time, and without callers getting an engaged signal on your phone line too. We have already seen that clogging up your telephone line while linked to the net via dial-up can deter clients. A broadband connection will enable you to work faster and more efficiently. If you shop around, you will be able to find a range of deals which can make broadband affordable, especially if you remember you will be able to work faster and more efficiently because of it.

Visit one or more of these websites to get up-to-date deals on broadband for your area:

- www.broadbandchecker.co.uk
- www.broadband-finder.co.uk
- www.moneysavingexpert.com

Setting up broadband
To get going with broadband, choose your Internet Service Provider (ISP) from one of the sites listed above. The ISP will arrange a start date to connect you. They will deliver what you need to get connected, possibly a modem, and a CD with step-by-step instructions.

Choosing your connection speed
For most people, a broadband connection of around 1Mb will be what you need to receive and send documents, and enjoy audio and video direct to your computer. While you may not think that audio and video are essential to your business, they are becoming more and more a part of business communications. You may be asked to write content for a company podcast, or copy for a webpage that will also include a company video. It will not help your business credibility if you cannot view the information that a client wants you to check out. A faster 2Mb+ connection should be chosen if you have more than one computer user linked up to the net at a time. This may be the case if you work with other free-

lancers or are thinking of taking on employees – or, of course, if you are working from your home and competing with a teenager who wants to play games online.

Printer

If you are using your computer for business, a printer is essential. From sending simple business letters to printing large reports from clients, you will be using your printer every day. If you choose a printer that gives good quality results, you can also create your own business stationery, which can be useful when starting up.

How to choose a printer

Think about how much use your printer will get. Domestic printers are really designed for low-volume, short-turnaround print jobs. They are, relatively speaking, slow, especially when compared to professional printing equipment. You will probably get thirty pages per minute at best. When choosing a printer, many will list their rate per minute for black and white text pages. For bigger jobs you will find it most cost effective to develop a working relationship with a good local printer.

Will you need to print in colour, and will the work you send out include images, illustrations or photographs? Print quality is measure in dots per inch (dpi). The greater number of dpi, the better your results will be. A printer that produces 300 dpi will be fine if most of your work is simply text, but a higher resolution, up to 1200 dpi will be better for logos, photographs, etc. Also consider whether you want to print solely on to A4 plain paper, or whether you need a printer that can handle a range of sizes, different paper finishes, envelopes, light card and more. In the world of PR, for example, it can be handy to be able to produce press information packs with a range of materials in them.

Look at the size of your printer too, and the space you have to house it. If it can be networked, will it have to be within reach of your router?

Inkjet or laser

The two main types of printer available to consumers and small businesses are inkjet and laser. These vary considerably in cost, speed and quality of results, so choose carefully. A laser printer will produce high-quality prints, with a good print speed, and a low cost-per-copy for black and white text. A good black and white laser printer can cost as little as £80 at the time of writing, while colour laser printers start in the region of £200. Watch out, as a low up-front price may not reflect the high cost of toner cartridges. *Which?* magazine says, 'If you need to print lots of colour documents quickly then you should look into getting a colour laser printer. Although these printers are initially more expensive than an inkjet they cost a lot less to run in the long run.' Another guide suggests a laser printer is best if you print more than a hundred pages of text each day. Colour quality is not as good as inkjets for printing photographs. Check the cost of supplies: toner cartridges can appear expensive, but you will get several thousand pages per cartridge.

Inkjet printers sold nowadays are mainly colour, and are good if you want to do a range of small print jobs, some in colour and some in black and white. In general the print quality for text won't be as high as with a laser printer, and you need to let the ink dry for a few seconds. There is also usually a higher cost per page as each cartridge will only produce between 50 and 300 pages. Check that your choice of printer comes with a colour and a black and white cartridge: colour cartridges are more expensive and it will save you enormously if you can opt for black and white only printing. Printing is slower than with a laser printer, and will vary within inkjet printers too. In *Which?* tests, the quickest inkjet printers produced five pages of plain black text in less than thirty seconds, while the slowest took more than eight minutes to perform the same task. While you can buy inkjet printers from as little as £20, a more expensive inkjet printer will give you better quality colour, can deliver more pages at a time, or can take heavier paper.

Printer supplies
You will now realize that as well as weighing up your options for a printer, you also need to take into account the cost of refills, or cartridges. In a *Which?* test, ink for an inkjet printer that cost just £30 came to about £580 for three years of moderate use. Check whether your choice of printer can only take refills from the manufacturer, or whether you can use third-party cartridges, which can be considerably cheaper. Quality can vary, so it may be a case of trying different cartridges and assessing the results.

At this point it is also worth mentioning paper quality. If you are delivering a professional service and sending articles or reports to clients in print, choosing a good quality paper can improve your presentation. It may be something as simple as choosing higher paper weight: 100 gsm can feel better than 80 gsm. Start looking at the sort of paper that documents you receive are printed on and use this to inform your choice of paper for your business.

More office technology

So far, it is clear that you will need a computer, phone and printer. That probably is not news to you, and with any luck you will have the necessary equipment to get started in your business writing enterprise. If you do not have your own computer, give your nearest enterprise agency a call as they will be able to help you find out about start-up grants. This sort of grant may depend on your age or your location, so unfortunately there are no guarantees.

Alongside the computer, telephone and printer, there are a number of other bits of office technology that can make your life easier, speed up communication with clients, and improve the professional service that you offer. A scanner, a photocopier and a fax can all be of use.

Scanners
A scanner can help you promote your business. If you get coverage for your own business, scan in features and display them on your website, after getting permission from the publication. Media

coverage can give potential clients confidence. If you are creating documents and reports for clients you may want to scan in images that you only have in print format. Scanning a document can save time if your software can recognize type and turn a scanned document into a Microsoft Word file, for example.

Fax

Though no longer an essential in every office, a fax is still useful. Credit and finance departments of many companies may ask for a signed agreement to be faxed through: if you have to post the agreement this can cause delays with products you are ordering. Many documents that would once have been faxed are now emailed, which is equally speedy and provides a high quality copy of the document for the recipient. Newspaper offices which would have once received hundreds of faxes now get press releases mostly by email.

You can get by without fax facilities, not least because it is possible to send and receive faxes via the internet. Internet fax services may want you to sign up for a monthly subscription, which may give you your own number to receive faxes. Plus points for having your own fax include the ability to feed in any document at your end, whereas if you use internet faxing facilities you will need a scanner to upload documents that require a signature. Many corner shops offer fax facilities, which are adequate if you want to send a fax, but less good for receiving unless you have a friendly shopkeeper. If you send several faxes the fees can mount up when using this sort of facility. A multifunction printer which is networked with your internet connection can save you having to buy a separate fax machine.

Photocopiers

A photocopier in your own office can be handy for creating a few copies of a document. Large commercial copiers cost thousands of pounds and purchase is usually out of the reach of small businesses and sole traders. There are a number of solutions to this, depending on the size and scale of what you want to replicate. If you have a scanner, single sheets can be scanned and then printed from a computer. A multifunction printer is a good solution for occasional copying needs. You may be able to use a photocopier in a local business centre or library: this is suitable for copying a few items but not cost effective for large print runs. For bigger projects involving tens or hundreds of copies or single documents with many pages, you are best finding a printer.

If copying documents turns out to be a regular part of your business you may want to look at leasing a business photocopier: lease agreements are usually for a number of years and cost from £60 per month, depending on the machine. Check whether your lease includes servicing, and do not forget to factor in the cost of printing supplies.

Multifunction printers
A multifunction printer can be the perfect solution for a sole trader running a writing business. Many such businesses do not require enormous amounts of scanning or photocopying, and you may find yourself needing to send faxes infrequently. Rather than investing in several pieces of equipment, a printer with scanner, copier and fax facilities can save you money, although of course will cost more than a regular printer. It will take up less space than having a separate fax, scanner and printer. Perhaps most importantly, having all the facilities in your workspace or home office will allow you to appear professional to clients.

When buying a multifunction printer (MFP), do check the print quality, as you don't want to gain more functions while losing dots per inch. For many multifunction printers, facilities can be used when your computer is switched off, meaning there is no need to get everything up and running when you want to copy one page or, assuming you have networked your MFP, when a fax comes in. Some multifunction printers include slots for media cards, allowing you to take images from a digital camera, say, straight to print.

There are a few negatives associated with MFPs, as well as the increased cost. You will need to send the whole unit for repair if one part fails, or indeed replace the whole unit. Check the size of the scanner bed as this may not be quite as large as a separate scanner unit. Larger scanner beds and built-in fax facilities tend to be included in the more expensive multifunction printers.

Interviews and recording equipment

If you are going to be interviewing people you may need recording equipment too. This can be useful if you are a copywriter, and is essential for a journalist. Making notes can be a useful back up for a recording, but the recording can allow you to concentrate on the interview without worrying you will miss something. You should also look for equipment that is compatible with your phone, for telephone interviews.

Choosing recording equipment

Your options include simple voice-activated tape recorders, mini-disc recorders or MP3 recorders. A tape recorder is a cheap option, starting from as little as £10. Some Dictaphones are suitable for one-to-one interviews in quiet environments; most will need an external microphone. A voice-operated recorder will start to record when you start talking.

There are lots of advantages to digital recordings. Recording quality is better, with fewer inaudible sections. Files can be downloaded and stored on your PC rather than on tapes which are easily lost or damaged. Recordings can be copied without losing quality. You can email a file for transcription. Digital recorders either use memory cards – different manufacturers have different size cards – or record on to an internal hard disc. Check out the length of recording which can be saved: some models can store a couple of hundred hours of recordings.

Minidisc recorders start from around £100, and are small and portable; there is some doubt over whether manufacturers will continue to produce this type of recorder, with few new models appearing now.

Digital recording files are large, so you will need broadband if you plan to send them by email, and plenty of storage space on your computer. A recorder with memory cards will allow you to make several recordings by simply replacing the card: one without will require you to download your files to your computer once its memory becomes full. More internal memory pushes up the price of digital recorders, which cost in the region of £100–£200: memory cards start from just a few pounds. Again, an external mic will provide much better recording quality.

Do not forget to check how your recording equipment, of whatever type, is powered. Rechargeable batteries can be the most cost-effective option if you need to use it out and about. For more tips on equipment and successful recordings see Chapter 9.

Back ups

Backing up your work is now essential. Your clients are relying on you, and your income depends on you being able to deliver the work you have agreed on deadline. Explanations such as 'my computer crashed' won't hold water, unless the client is incredibly understanding, and who wants to repeat a whole load of work anyway? There are a number of options available to help you back up your work.

Starting simply, if you are working on a big project, save a copy of your work as you go somewhere other than on the primary hard drive on your main computer. You could back up your documents to disc, to a zip or flash drive or to a second hard drive, or to another computer. You can get as much as 5Gb on a disc, and far more on to an external hard drive. Check whether your computer has a CD RW or DVD RW drive as this will allow you to burn the information to disc. If you have a rewrite drive this is a simple and affordable way to back up. If you don't, these drives can be purchased and installed on most computers, and you will find them useful for writing information to disc to send to clients.

Make back ups in a way that you can keep them in a separate location: this helps if your computer is stolen, for example, or if your office is flooded. A second hard drive in your computer is vulnerable to a power surge or virus which affects your main hard drive, while removable storage or an online back up would not be affected.

Regular back ups

There are facilities on most computers to remind you to make regular back ups, or you can get this included with computer protection software like Norton. This will take a copy of everything on your computer, including your emails, work files, applications and operating system. This lets you reinstall everything in the event of disaster. Whichever way you do it, back up on a regular and frequent basis: I'm backing up while writing this as researching this section has reminded me how important it is.

Online back ups

There are many companies offering services which allow you to back up your data online. It is then stored safely, in a location away from your own home or office, reducing the chances of disaster. Uploading data for back up can be time consuming, even if you have a broadband connection. Services charge a monthly or annual fee.

Shopping and saving

Interestingly, there is a season for buying tech equipment. *Which?* magazine reports that it is best to shop in August or September to take advantage of 'back to college' deals aimed at students. While this advice will not help if you need to make a purchase in the other ten months, you can make sure you get the best deal by checking prices on the internet at sites like Pricerunner or Kelkoo. For all your technology needs, shop around, read reviews, and take a little time rather than making a snap decision which could end up being a costly mistake.

Chapter 2

Skills you will need

If you are planning a career in commercial writing, it is important to ensure you have the right skills to start off with. Work out the sort of work you want to do, and look at the qualifications, skills and knowledge you need to be successful. If you are clear on your strengths you can:

- take courses to help with your weaker areas;
- be clear about what sort of work will suit you, and what you can do well;
- be able to sell your strong points to potential clients.

This chapter will take you through the skills, knowledge, qualifications and experience that can help you on your way to a full-time writing business.

Your skills

Copywriting
The key skill for many commercial writing careers is copywriting. If you're unsure exactly what copywriting is, think of it as writing to promote something. Copywriting is used on paper, on the net, on TV and on the radio. You could be promoting an individual, a

business, a product or ideas. The main idea is that you use your skills to write persuasive text which will make people think in a certain way, make them desire something, or make them say yes to a request or opportunity.

Copywriting skills are essential for work in advertising or PR. They help when you are developing leaflets or other promotional materials for business clients. You could use copywriting skills to help a client with branding, taglines and slogans. A writer with good copywriting skills can find work creating catalogues or sales letters, annual reports or fundraising materials. You might find yourself paid to write an advertorial (an article written for inclusion in a newspaper or magazine in a space paid for by the advertiser) for a company that wants something more detailed to sell the benefits of its business in the local paper.

The internet has led to a growing role for copywriters who understand search-engine optimization, the art of using key words to ensure a website is picked up on relevant searches, while at the same time ensuring the content is readable and accessible for site users.

Copywriting skills
Do you know what makes good copy? Maybe you are moving from a career in another sector and want to start to build your writing skills from scratch. Here are some key pointers to help you assess your own writing skills, and see if you have what it takes to get started in the writing business.

What is the objective?
Can you write with a point in mind? When you are commissioned to write for a business, they will have something that they need the copy to achieve. They may be clear about this, but if not it will be up to you to draw out their aims and clarify them. Think about whether you know how to set a clear objective for your writing, and then have the skills to meet that objective.

Do you know how to assess your target audience?
When you are commissioned to do some commercial writing, you need to know who you are writing for. Different audiences require

different approaches, different lengths and styles. You need to be able to talk to clients and find out who they want your writing to reach. The more you know about your potential target audience, the better you can tailor your writing. If you want to find out more, look at media packs for magazines, for example. They can tell you who reads the publication, and may have data on their habits, education, profession, income and lifestyle too. Develop the skills to get a clear picture in your head of who you are writing for.

Can you write in different and appropriate styles?

Do you have the skills to write in different ways for different audiences? If you are writing a leaflet about a product aimed at new parents, remember that they are sleep-deprived and unlikely to get more than two minutes to themselves to read something. The same company might have also commissioned you to write about the product for midwives and health visitors. How would you make the content different from the parents' leaflet? Think about the health professionals' level of education, time and availability for reading and pattern of work. Focus on your reader's needs to help you hone your approach.

How would you structure a document?

Do you just put pen to paper, or fingers to keyboard, and write? That approach may work well for creative writing, fiction and poetry, but it is different for business writing. A good copywriter will know how to structure a document for the best effect. If you are sending a press release, you need to grab the journalist's attention with the title and possibly the first line. A compelling article should have a beginning that makes people want to read on. If you have complex data to get across you need to be able to break it down into digestible sections, to keep readers reading. And if you are writing a sales letter, do you know how to turn the ending into a compelling call to action?

Features and benefits

One of the main skills in writing copy that works to sell products and services is being able to identify the benefits. Whenever you approach a writing job, get to know the topic you are covering. Your client may have plenty of information on what is great about what they offer, or you may need to develop some ideas for them to look at. The main thing is to focus on how you can solve a problem for the reader or improve their life.

Other, more technical, writing may require you to be very factual. You could be developing a user guide or brochure. Do you have the skills to assess the sort of writing you are doing, and make the content fit the job? You may want to focus on persuasive copywriting or become a technical copywriting whizz. Alternatively, some copywriters like to be versatile to maximize their opportunities.

Research skills

Some clients may supply you with everything you need to write their materials. In other situations, perhaps when writing a piece for a newspaper, it is entirely up to you to research the content. What are your research skills like? Are you at home with online searching? Do you know how to use libraries or get in touch with the bodies that hold the information you need? Are you up to date on the Freedom of Information Act?

How do you know what you write works?

When you write something for a client, they will want your words to have a specific effect. How do you know what that effect will be? A focus group can give you the chance to get feedback from 'real' readers, and check that you are achieving your client's aims and objectives. While not every writer needs to be able to run focus groups to try out what they have written on users, it is helpful to know if and when a piece of copy should be tested. If you are creating a direct mail campaign that will go to millions of homes, how will you know that the messages you have written will give the right outcome?

Can you write persuasively?

A good copywriter needs to be able to appeal to the reader's emotions, and not only when writing fundraising letters for charities. You need to be able to sell tools to builders, shoes to fashionistas, new IT set-ups to the person responsible for purchasing decisions – you get the idea. And what works for one group won't necessarily hit the buttons you need to push for others. As I explained above, it helps if you have a clear idea of your target reader. This will help you develop a rapport, understand their motivation, select the appropriate tone and style for the reader and topic and know what words will appeal to them.

Can you adapt?

Do you have the skills to make your words work for the job in hand, and adapt quickly as each new job needs? Working in-house you may have been used to sticking with one project. As a freelancer you can be juggling several clients. You need a sharp mind to shift from one style of writing to another: your income can depend on it.

Are you good at grammar?

If you are about to set forth on a copywriting career, whether you want to work in new media, run your own PR business or freelance for big advertising agencies, you need to have a sound grasp of grammar and spelling. It is not acceptable to pick this up as you go along. Clients are paying you for accurate writing. Typos (a mistake in typing or printing) and bad grammar will damage your reputation and stop clients returning. What is more, there are good reasons for good grammar. Structuring sentences in a consistent way, in line with people's expectations, makes them far easier to read. Good grammar can help you get your client's message across.

There are plenty of good grammar guides. Do not be afraid to check words as you write. Have a dictionary handy. Do not rely on spell check. It will pick up some errors, but can let you down if you have simply substituted 'of' for 'or', for example. Work out your own way of proofing your output. If you share an office, could you agree to read through a colleague's work in return for them checking yours? If you work by yourself, print out your copy to check it. You may find you pick up more errors if you leave a short while between writing and checking, or even return to check the document the next day. Of course, this is hard when you are on a deadline, a time when even the most accurate writer can find silly errors slipping in.

If you want to improve your grammar, and make sure you have the right skills to be confident when delivering copy, see the Appendix at the end of the book.

Readability

One further factor that you need to consider is the readability of your text. It is hard to track down the source of the suggestion that the average UK adult has the reading age of a nine-year-old, but whether this is accurate or not, it has an important message for copywriters. If you have embarked on a writing career, you are probably pretty literate, more so than most people. Keep what you are writing simple and more people will be able to read it. Making your text easy to read means people understand it, can read it more rapidly, retain more of what you have written, and are more likely to read to the end. The clarity of your text will depend on the length of your sentences and the number of syllables in the words that you use. If you want to run a specific test on something you have written, look up Flesch–Kincaid tests or the Fry Readability formula. These formulae will give you a reading age or school grade that would be able to read your copy, though they are not 100 per cent accurate and should be seen only as a guide. You may find it more helpful to learn by example. Look at the website of the Campaign for Plain English, www.plainenglish.co.uk, and check out some of their 'before and after' examples of long-winded writing and their own short, clear alternatives. In your writing, try to use short words, and break down sentances with good punctuation. If something looks as though it is beginning to get complicated, can you make it clear? This is a vital skill for anyone hoping to sell their writing skills.

House style

One further note: some clients will want you to write in their house style. Before you start a job, save yourself time and ask if they have a style guide. This will set out when to use numerals and when to write numbers in full, for example, alongside information on when and how to use capitals and accents.

If you want to find out more about style, publications like *The Guardian* and *The Economist* publish style guides, both of which you can find online:

- www.economist.com/research/StyleGuide
- www.guardian.co.uk/styleguide

Also look at *The Elements of Style* by William Strunk and E.B. White.

Can you create original copy?

When you are writing for a living you need to be a fount of originality and new ideas. Clients won't be happy if you come up with the same approach for everyone. If you want to get features or news ideas accepted, you need to have a new take on an old subject at the very least. To generate coverage for a press release, you have to tell the journalist about the new and unique angles they could use. If you are wondering whether you can get the same buzz out of copywriting as you can out of writing for pleasure, I think most copywriters would say you can. There is the same need for creativity, you should still have the same passion for writing, and you will need the same ability to play with words until you have a piece of copy just right.

It is not always easy to keep up a high level of originality. Pedantic readers can probably go back through this page and find ten places where I could have been more original. Even as I write this, trite phrases are trying to trip off my tongue. Develop some resources for inspiration. Keep a thesaurus on your desk. It can help you find new ways to say the same thing, and avoid clichés.

People skills

Business writers who make a decent living are not just great writers; they have to be good with people too. Ask yourself whether you are happy to pick up the phone to a potential client, and persuade them you are right for the job. There are lots of ways to make it easier. Practise your phone call, write a script with key questions and answers. You do not have to stick to it rigidly, but a script can help you feel confident.

And if it comes to a meeting, can you tell the client about your skills or assess their needs and outline how you can help in a clear and confident manner? If you are unsure about this, remember that it just takes practice. When you are meeting clients, dressing well can help you feel good. Again, preparation can make you confident that you can handle anything.

Key skills checklist

You probably have more skills than you realize: read through this list and note which areas you feel confident in and those where you might need some help.

- Do you know how to assess who you are writing for?
- Can you write in different and appropriate styles?
- Can you structure a document?
- Can you write persuasive text or follow facts?
- Have you got good research skills?
- Can you write persuasively?
- Are you confident about your grammar and spelling?
- Can you create original copy?
- Are you confident on the phone and in face-to-face meetings?

As well as writing skills there are other abilities that will smooth your transition to being a business writer. Look at Chapter 3 to get an idea of the skills you need to run a successful business. The suggestions in this book can only start you off on the road to becoming a copywriter. As you read it you will find lots more resources to follow up and help you learn and improve. Read the rest of this chapter and the following ones for more details of courses to help you keep your skills fresh, and develop areas where you are weaker. The better you know your strong points, the more able you are to focus your work on your strengths and to sell your skills to potential clients.

The *Media Directory* (Guardian Books) has a list of universities offering media courses, divided into sections including 'general media', press, journalism and writing, PR marketing and advertising, publishing and multimedia.

Your knowledge

In one way, a copywriter or business writer does not need to have specific knowledge: your job is to take information from your client, and turn it into compelling copy. However, if you have a specialist area of knowledge this can help you sell your skills to a niche market. Clients can find you indispensable if you do not need time to get up to speed in their area of business.

On the other hand, the better you know your business, the more convincing you will be to potential clients. If you are looking to break into feature writing, read the publications you want to target. If you want to work in advertising, make it part of your everyday routine to look critically at adverts and slogans. Become a critical consumer of websites if you want to get into creating online content. Reading can really help you become a better writer. Everywhere I go I assess slogans and taglines. I cast a critical eye over press releases I receive. Maybe I can learn something from someone else's great writing, or spot errors to avoid in the future. If you have a passion for your area of work, this can be a pleasure. It is also something that can take over your life, and turn a passion into a pain. I need to have a good knowledge of women's magazines when I am doing PR, which has taken the pleasure out of relaxing with a coffee and a magazine: it is no longer a way to switch off from work.

Essential knowledge – the law

If you are setting out to do any sort of writing for profit, you need to know your law. This does not mean that you need a legal degree, but, depending on the sort of work you do, you should have a firm grip on copyright and libel. Frances Quinn, freelance journalist and author of *Law for Journalists* (Pearson 2007) says:

> If you're writing copy on behalf of a company, you're clearly unlikely to be risking a defamation claim from them, because they'll have approved everything you write. But don't let that lull you into a false sense of security, because the fact that the company has approved the copy doesn't let you off the hook if, for example, the copy libels a competitor with false comparisons to your client. People often think that the libel laws only apply to journalism, but in fact they apply to absolutely any material that is published, whether on the internet, in brochures or leaflets, ads or point of sale material. Publication in this sense simply means conveying the words to someone other than the person they are about, or that person's spouse, so for example, if you libel someone in a press release, you can be liable simply for sending out the release to magazines and newspapers, even if none of them publishes the information in it. And even if they do, you, and/or your client, could be liable alongside them.
>
> Although a copywriter is unlikely to be sued personally, it's important to realize that technically, you could be. And of course, even if only the client is sued, it doesn't reflect well on you personally and is unlikely to do your copywriting career much good.
>
> You might expect, especially if you're working for a big company, that they'll have their own lawyers to check everything, but unless the people commissioning the material from you are aware of media law (and often they're not), they may not even realize that seemingly innocuous marketing material could raise legal issues, and so they won't refer it to the lawyers. That's why, as a writer, you need to have enough knowledge to realize when there's a legal issue to consider.

Copyright

Anything that you write is your copyright, unless you have signed a contract to assign the right to a client. No one else has the right to copy what you have created, and no one can use it without your permission. Copyright protects writing, designs and illustrations, photographs and cartoons, music and content you have created for the internet. It also applies to the spoken word so, if you are record-ing an interview, the interviewee has copyright for what he or she said. You should ask permission to record any interview, and need to get permission to take quotes from the recording. Copyright does not always protect ideas: if you pitch a feature to a magazine and then something along the same lines appears a few months later, you do not have legal comeback.

You do not need to make a specific record of your work for copyright purposes or register it with anybody, but keeping research and source material or dated notes and sketches can be evidence of when you came up with the piece of work if there is a copyright infringement.

The copyright symbol, ©, is not essential to protect your work, in UK law, but can remind clients about how they use what you have written. This is different in the US where work protected by the American Copyright Statute must include 'copyright' or ©, your name and the year of publication.

You need to be clear in any contract for work whether you are retaining the copyright and letting the client have use of what you have written for a specific purpose, or assigning copyright to the client to use the text in any way they want. Get legal advice on setting up contracts and see the Copyright, Designs and Patents Act 1988.

Plagiarism

Copyright law means that others may not copy your work. Plagiarism is when you copy all or part of someone else's work without permission. If you need to quote an extract, you should get permission from the copyright owner. Copyright lasts for seventy years after the author's death, so you still need to get permission.

Libel and slander

Libel occurs when you defame someone in writing, so may be an issue you need to be aware of in your writing business. The work needs to have been published, which can simply mean sent to a third party. Someone can claim libel when you have injured their reputa0tion, in permanent form. Slander is the verbal publication of defamatory material. To prove slander, someone usually needs to demonstrate that they have suffered a financial loss.

More law
There is only the space to give you some basic information on areas of law which will affect your work here. There is some information on this in the *Writers' and Artists' Yearbook*. For full coverage of the topic, read *McNae's Essential Law for Journalists* or *Law for Journalists* (OUP, 2007) by Frances Quinn. If you want to spend more time studying the subject you could take a media law course like those run by the National Council for the Training of Journalists, or look at joining an organization like the NUJ who offer short courses on 'Copyright for Journalists'. See www.nctj.com and www.nujtraining.org.uk. Organizations like the NUJ and the Society of Authors will assist members with legal, contract and copyright queries.

Your qualifications

What qualifications do you have, and will they help you in your career as a commercial writer? To start with, if you do not have a formal writing qualification, don't panic. There are lots of people working as writers without certificates. This does not mean that you can be successful without some key skills: what it does mean is that being able to create compelling and accurate copy is more important than whether you have a degree in English Literature.

If you want to improve your qualifications, why not start by looking at the professional body for the sector you want to get into? In each chapter in the later part of this book, there are details of the professional bodies for careers including advertising, marketing, PR and journalism. Each professional body should be able to point you in the direction of recognized courses. The British Association of Communicators in Business (www.cib.uk.com, 01908 313755) offers a great range of courses if you want to brush up a skill, from 'effective writing' to headline writing, editing and proofreading. The National Union of Journalists offers courses in professional skills: for example, feature writing, online publishing, and the use of relevant computer software.

If you want to look locally, or find a distance learning course, start by searching Learn Direct (www.learndirect.co.uk). Not all courses are equal, so it pays to do your research. Get a prospectus, and see which body has accredited or validated the course. Check what the college is claiming: if possible speak to the tutor and current students. Find data on what former students are doing now. The Open & Distance Learning Quality Council is a voluntary regulation scheme for distance learning providers.

Your experience

To break into any sort of copywriting on a freelance or self-employed basis, you need experience. The more work you have to show to potential clients the more likely they are to have confidence in your ability to take on their work.

No experience?
Do some networking and see if there is someone else starting up in business who might want to swap skills. When I started my PR business, I worked with a woman who started a web design company: I helped her promote her business and she created my website. You can find contacts at your local enterprise agency which will run business start-up sessions, your local chamber of commerce, and online business networking sites like UK Business Forums.

If you have been working in a compatible industry, see if you can use your contacts, maybe put in a few extra hours, and work your way into a position to get some of the right sort of experience. Take a look at the work you have done: is there anything that could be relevant to potential clients? Even if it isn't exactly the same as the services you are going to offer, some of your previous work may display your writing skills.

Your portfolio

A portfolio of work you have done can be just what you need to convince clients. If you are currently employed and want to widen your experience and portfolio, try to build up some freelance work in your spare time, while you can still rely on your salary to pay the bills. If you want to work in advertising or be part of a creative team in marketing, a portfolio showcasing your work on other marketing campaigns or adverts is vital.

Clients

If you are already working in the sector where you hope to go freelance, be careful about how you go about getting clients. Your contract may prevent you doing work for businesses that are already using your employer's services. This can seem frustrating. Many freelancers have started careers using contacts from work without repercussions, but do check your own situation first. You don't have to poach clients to get started. Use networking contacts to find other businesses who might want some work done.

Self-promotion

Get over any embarrassment about telling people what you do. If you do not promote your services, who else will do it for you? Develop a short sentence to sum up what you offer. Make sure you highlight your unique skills and strong points. Practise saying it to yourself or to a friend and get their feedback on how it sounds. Ask them what stood out to them. Refine what you say until you feel confident that you are able to sell your business skills. If someone you do not know well says 'So what do you do?' in a social situation, the words describing your writing business should roll off your tongue. They may have a business and be looking for a copywriter, or know someone who is.

Building your portfolio

In the beginning, you may not have an enormous number of pieces of work, and want to include everything in a portfolio. If you have been writing for a while, you may have a stack of hundreds of cuttings in a heap on your desk or a folder of scanned files and pdfs on your computer. Whatever your situation, take some time to look critically at what you have available to help win new clients and convince them of your skills.

Using your portfolio

Clients will often want to see an example of your work so that they can see what you do. You may want to have a website with examples of your work (see below) or need to send work to a client by email or post. Having a supply of previous work available can help clinch a contract, but you need to apply your judgement to what you send.

First, go through your work with a critical eye, and pull out the pieces you are proud of and pleased by. If you have work that you are less than happy with, you are unlikely to want to show it to clients. Then, sift through your cuttings and see how they fit with the sort of work you are hoping to get. If you have had enough of low-paid writing for the local paper and are hoping to get some more lucrative contracts for business writing, select any pieces which show how you have taken a client's information and turned it into a brochure, advert or leaflet. This may be more relevant than the hundreds of articles you have produced. If you feel you do not have enough cuttings in the right area, create some. There might be a charity or group nearby which would be grateful for some help with copywriting. They get the help they need, and you get the work to add to your portfolio.

Relevant and timely

Do not just have a standard portfolio that you send to every enquirer. However much you may feel that one piece of work is your best advertisement, it is unlikely to be right for every potential client. Choose pieces of work that show similar skills to those you would be using in the job you are pitching for. You may want something that is written for a similar target audience or in a relevant style. You should also ensure that you are sending out relatively recent pieces of work. Clients are less likely to be impressed by work from many years ago. If you have had a career break, see the tips above for getting experience and use them to generate some more current examples of work to boost your portfolio.

Displaying your portfolio

Remember that your portfolio is a vital tool in promoting your writing skills. Make sure that whatever you show to clients is professionally presented. Much of the time it can be an advantage to be able to send cuttings and examples by email. The recipient will get your portfolio faster, while their mind is still on the project, and you can steal a march on slower competitors.

Think about the quality of the files that you send: a high resolution image may be a better advertisement for your work than a low resolution one, but you may need to check that your potential client can accept a large file. If you have a very visual portfolio, with a focus on design and branding, you may want to send this by mail or link to your website instead.

If you need to scan in cuttings or examples of your work, make sure that the scans are aligned correctly, so the final result looks as good as possible. When working on projects in the future, ask for several copies of any brochures or leaflets that contain your work. Ideally ask for a pdf to save you having to scan articles in the future.

Testimonials

Alongside the examples of your work, it is helpful to have client comments. If a client has said something spontaneously on completion of some work, ask if you can use the comment. Similarly, if they have emailed to say that you did a good job, see if you can include that alongside the relevant piece of work. Don't be embarrassed to ask people how they feel the project has gone. You may get some good feedback, and you can use what they say to improve your service as well as for generating testimonials.

Your portfolio online

An online portfolio is a great way to generate work and new clients. If you have a clear description of what you offer and the benefits of using your services on a website, clients will find your details if they search online. You can find clients approaching you rather than having to do all the legwork to generate work for yourself. If you are going to put cuttings and examples of previous work online it is courteous to always ask the client, and provide a link to their business. If they have the copyright for the work you need to ask their permission.

Setting up a website

It is not hard to set up a simple website to act as an online portfolio and advertisement for your writing business. Buy a relevant domain name; www.yourname.co.uk or www.yourbusinessname.co.uk can be a good place to start. You can buy domain names from lots of different companies: search online to find one. You may have some hosting provided with your internet service, or you could buy a website set-up from a company which will provide you with hosting and a choice of templates for you to customize. You could also choose to use a blog, which is already set up and hosted for you. You have the same opportunity to customize the way it looks, and a blog is well designed for displaying your cuttings and adding new content which displays your writing skills. See Chapter 4 for more ways to use a website to boost your business and find new clients.

The next steps

If you have worked through this chapter, you should have a good idea of whether you are ready to start a career as a commercial writer. If you have spotted an obvious weak point, you may be able to address it by practising your skills or taking a short course. If you are lacking experience, spend a few weeks making contacts and creating some examples of your work. A course can help with this too.

Tracey Dooley
Tracey 'Word Doctor' Dooley is a creative consultant and business writer. She started making a living with words in 1993 and set up

her business, MediaMinister.co.uk, in 2001. Tracey's work is full of variety. She says:

> No two days are the same. One day I might be working on some rigorous technical report, the next I'll be developing a marketing plan for someone selling horse gear. That said, I do have certain tasks I carry out each and every day, like checking my emails, and responding to urgent ones. I then look at my 'To Do' list for that day, and prioritize. My clients range from start-up 'one-woman-bands' to blue-chip companies. I love the variety that that brings. As well as offering editorial and marketing consultation, I write and edit blogs, websites, direct response materials, reports, brochures, articles, books, educational tools. . . . You name it; I've probably turned my hand to it.

Tracey enjoys the freedom of working for herself and writing full time. She says:

> Being my own boss, and being able to work to my own timetable, was and still is a big plus. Also, not having to commute and the distinct lack of office politics rate highly on the 'self-employment pros' front. The negatives include solitude, being my own boss (I can be quite hard on myself at times!) and unpaid holidays. If I am being brave and honest, I do find the business side (especially taxes) a real bother. As for the writing side, I love getting great feedback from clients; it really does make it all worthwhile. I find the creative brainstorming on jobs such as creating taglines and brand names a real boon. Also, the variety in both workload and clientele is thoroughly inspiring. And, of course, being able to satisfy the creative side of me through writing is a bonus. The negatives of writing include the fact that not everyone values the role of copywriting: everyone thinks they can write. Perhaps the biggest challenge is when someone asks me to write an entire website for £50! I have over the years realized that the client who shops on price alone is not one worth having — they are often more trouble than their job is worth.

Chapter 3

Business basics

If you want to write for a living, you need to be aware of how to set up a business. You should understand the basic legal requirements. This chapter looks at clarifying the basis on which you will work, and covers important issues such as money, tax and insurance. You can also find out about contracts and fees, and where to get more advice. When you work for yourself, you are responsible for all aspects of the business. Joanne Mallon says, 'Remember that running a writing business involves many other skills than just being a good writer. You will also need to be a salesperson, negotiator, interviewer, typist, bookkeeper, office cleaner, etc. Take a holistic approach and sharpen up on your skills besides writing.' This chapter will help you find out more.

Registering as self-employed

When you become self-employed, you need to register with the Inland Revenue. This applies whether you plan to freelance in another business's office, or are setting up your own business of any kind. You have a duty to do this within three months of becoming self-employed, or you will be liable for a fine. You are self-employed if you carry out work for a number of clients, and invoice them for it, are responsible for your business's profits and losses, and have control over when and how the work is done. There are other factors which will help you determine if you are self-employed, such as whether you provide your own equipment. Remember that you can be self-employed even if you also have a day job with an employer.

Louisa Bird of the Women's Marketing Forum says, 'Being self-employed is by no means the easy route. I was always determined to work freelance. The freedom and flexibility can't be beaten. But you should take time to be really clear about your specialization, the sort of people you want to work with and what you enjoy doing most. You will need persistence and determination to succeed.'

Most writers will start off as a sole trader, and the majority will carry on working this way. Some people may decide it is beneficial financially to set their business up as a company, but this also brings more responsibilities.

Sole traders

Sole traders pay tax through the self-assessment system. You will also need to pay Class 2 National Insurance contributions of a few pounds a week, even if you are working on an employed basis as well. These flat-rate payments go towards a basic state pension, and incapacity, maternity and bereavement benefits. If you earn a small amount you may be able to claim exemption from National Insurance contributions, but it can be worth paying anyway to ensure you get the benefits should you need them. You can pay weekly or monthly by direct debit, or by quarterly bill. You also need to pay Class 4 NI on income over a certain level. Check with the Inland Revenue for current figures.

Setting up a company

You may decide to set up your business as a company for a number of reasons. Setting up a company will keep your personal and business finances separate. You won't be liable for a company's debts, which cuts your personal risk, unless you have given a guarantee for a loan, for example. It can be easier to get finance and loans as a company, or sell the business on. This is probably more relevant if you see yourself running a PR or advertising agency than if you want to write features, although some writers operate as a company. If you set up a company your business's financial records have to be publicly available through Companies House. Profits from a company are distributed to shareholders as a dividend. Get advice from an accountant on whether this will be of more benefit to you: you can end up paying less tax this way, depending on current tax legislation.

Ian Murphy works as a sole trader, and has a limited company for other aspects of his work. Ian explains:

> Under the self-employed status I currently do a series of white papers for HP, some writing for IT Pro, some lab work for various third party companies and other general writing. With the limited company I publish some small press magazines and manage their websites. I also put the work I do for any analyst companies such as Phillips Global Media and Ovum through the limited company. This is because there is more risk due to the contracts that I sign for analysts than those for normal computer journalism. What a lot of self-employed people miss out is that a limited company if properly structured is a much better vehicle for anything that might risk your house. Provided you have shown that you are acting correctly, the limited company as a separate legal entity is no risk to your home. As self-employed, you can quickly find yourself with too close a mix between business and personal and that leaves you open to serious debt problems should you get it wrong.

You can create your own company and register it at Companies

House, or buy a ready-made company from an agent. If you decide to turn your business into a company, you have various duties. You must:

- display the full corporate name outside your business premises;
- display your corporate registration details on the company stationery;
- file statutory documents, such as accounts and annual returns.

Corporation tax is charged on company profits, but you become a company employee, and are therefore paid after the company has deducted Class 1 National Insurance and PAYE tax. You also need to be registered for self-assessment.

A private limited company must have one shareholder, while a public limited company needs two, and must make shares available to the public. It is no longer necessary to have a company secretary.

See an accountant or solicitor for advice on what will work best in your particular circumstances. You need to be prepared to pay for this professional help if you want to work under a company set-up, and need to feel confident with a certain amount of form filling.

Andy Turner has been writing for a living for more than twenty years. He says:

> I started out working in marketing for BT, reporting for, and later editing, the company house journal. During this period, I took a Communication, Advertising and Marketing (CAM) Foundation qualification at Trinity and All Saints College in Leeds. Later on, when I moved into PR consultancy, I used the corporate journalism skills honed at BT to write for all kinds of magazines, newsletters, sales collateral, white papers, annual reports, websites, etc.

Andy became self-employed by 1998, and set up a limited company in 2000. He says:

An accountant recommended trading through a company structure for financial and personal, professional liability reasons. I traded as Six Sigma Public Relations Ltd until 2006, when I relocated to France. The benefits were numerous. The greatest was that I paid less tax, as my earnings were structured around the then lower tax treatment applied to dividend payments. At the time it was 10 per cent, although it has risen significantly since then. My wife was a co-director and so we were able to put in place legal tax avoidance measures that allowed us to keep more of our earnings than we would otherwise have been able to do. The limited company status lowered our personal liabilities in the event of any legal actions from clients: fortunately, there weren't any. Some clients prefer, and some insist, that sole trader suppliers operate through a limited company to lower the chance of 'disguised employment' investigations by Customs and Revenue interest under IR35 regs. In some clients' eyes, it makes you look more professional and perhaps more established.

Andy has some tips for anyone thinking of running a business:

Find good advisers and be prepared to pay them well. They will save you money in the long run. Keep business and personal money completely separate. Open a business account, plus a linked high interest deposit account, and trade through this. Build and retain capital. You will earn good interest on it in your deposit account and it will tide you over the inevitable lean times. Be commercial: always know what the going rate is, charge appropriately according to your skills and experience (so many people undercharge), operate under and enforce strict thirty-day credit terms, because cash flow is critical, especially early on. When you reach the VAT registration threshold, look closely at applying for both the annual accounting and flat-rate schemes; these saved me a considerable amount of administration and tax over several years.

Finances and insurance

Before you get much further, take some time to think about tax and insurance. These are unlikely to be the parts of working for yourself that excite and inspire you, but sorting them out at the start will save you headaches, time and expense later on.

Insurance

A writer needs to insure himself or herself for a number of reasons. If you provide work for a client that is factually inaccurate this could cost the client money. An error in a catalogue or brochure could lead to thousands of copies needing to be reprinted. Something you wrote could even lead to legal action, and you need insurance to cover yourself for the cost of legal fees and possibly damages.

Take a look at your office, and tot up just how much your equipment would cost if you had to replace it. This is another good reason to take out insurance today. Once you begin a career as a commercial writer, your income and home can depend on you being able to work. A flood or burglary may be devastating if you are employed, but if you are self-employed it can prevent you earning your living.

If you work from home, look at your insurance policy. Give the company a call and explain that you are now using your computer for work. Depending on the company and the amount and type of work that you do they may still be happy to cover you. However, you may get better and more appropriate cover from a business policy. You might want to look for a policy that will cover a laptop or camera if it gets stolen while you are out on a job, and will cover the hire of replacements so you can keep working if your computer has a breakdown.

Be warned that in some cases an insurance firm may withdraw cover altogether if you are working from home, and a home insurance policy will not cover loss of stock, such as samples belonging to a client, or if a client has an accident on your property.

If you work from a shared office or your own business premises you may need a few different types of insurance policy. With a shared office, check with the person or organization you have an agreement with about what is covered by their insurance.

If you take out a business property policy, you can get insurance for your own equipment, fixtures and fittings, plus cover for leased equipment and clients' property. You will also need to have public liability insurance if clients come to your premises. This covers legal fees, costs and expenses and damages if someone is injured while in your office.

Insurance for staff

If you have staff, you also need employer's liability compulsory insurance to meet the costs of compensation and legal fees for employees who are injured or made ill at work through the fault of the employer. You do not need this insurance if you are the only employee of a company, nor if you are a self-employed sole trader.

Professional indemnity insurance

This type of policy protects you if you have made mistakes or have been negligent in some of the services you provide to clients. It will cover you for legal costs and compensation. You can find general policies for small businesses, as well as more specific policies for writers. You need to arrange cover before you start work, and need to ensure that your cover is continuous, so you have cover for when the problem occurred, and when the client actually makes the claim, which may be years down the line.

Professional organizations can help you find the right cover, and may have links with insurance companies which specialize in insurance for writers. For example, the NUJ has worked with an insurance company to come up with a policy that covers members' costs in defending cases which involve libel and slander, infringement of copyright, breach of confidentiality, negligence, and liability to the public. Look at Chapter 5 onwards for details of the professional body relevant to your different areas of work. If you are looking for an insurance company, check that they are a member of the Association of British Insurers.

Setting up your finances

Think about whether you need a separate business bank account. If you are operating as a company you have no choice: a business bank account is compulsory. If you are a self-employed sole trader, there are still benefits. It can be easier to see your business expenditure and income with a separate account. You will also find it simpler to pay all business expenses from a separate account rather than paying expenses from your own pocket and then reckoning up afterwards. As a sole trader you can simply draw down the amount you need each month from the business. If you are running a company you need to pay yourself a salary: an accountant or bookkeeper can help you set up a simple payroll system. There are several low-cost or fee-free business accounts available from a good number of banks.

Patricia, a journalist, says:

> The money side of things takes up a great deal of time and is very tedious. When I was a sole trader I was logging every bus ticket and book purchase. It's very boring but very necessary. We've had our UK accountant since the dawn of time and he's a godsend. You do have to allow for bad debt every few years or so. Not getting paid is a pain: I once had to threaten three separate clients with court action in the course of a year. I would suggest to anyone who's thinking of being a freelance writer, sort your finances out first. Pay off your mortgage if you can, and have six months' earnings in the bank before you start, otherwise you'll always be coming from behind financially. The fewer outgoings you have, the less income you will need.

Money and record-keeping

Before you get too many months into your writing career, take some time out to plan how you will keep a record of what you spend on the business and what you earn. Good records of income and outgoings have many advantages. You can see where the profits are coming from; which clients are most profitable; which payments are overdue; and check that you are making enough to pay your bills. You are allowed to claim various business expenses against tax, but need to keep receipts in case you are inspected by the Inland Revenue. And without good records it can be nigh on impossible to fill in your end-of-year tax return. While accountants can give you plenty of essential business advice, hiring one to sort out a big pile of receipts, invoices and the like is a costly way to meet your duty to get your self-assessment form in on time. Either enter your income and expenses as you incur them throughout the year, or find a bookkeeper who will, for an affordable fee, keep your books up to date on a regular basis. If you don't meet the deadline to submit your tax return you can end up paying a fine.

What records to keep?

- Receipts for business buys.
- Travel receipts and tickets.
- Records of subscriptions.
- Receipts for membership fees for professional organizations.
- Copies of invoices to clients.
- Bank statements – print out a copy of online statements and add to your files.
- Building society books.
- Details of cash expenses.
- Any investment into the business.
- Suppliers' bills.
- Utility bills.
- Payslips from current or former jobs.

Keep records for at least five years from the date you submit your tax return.

Tools to help you keep records

It is up to you how you want to keep a record of your business finance. You may want to start simply with a book to record income and expenditure: a spreadsheet can do much the same but has the advantage of tools to help you get your sums right. Beyond that, you might want to purchase an accounts programme like Sage or Quickbooks. The advantage of a specific piece of software like this is that it can help you run your business, providing the facility to create and track invoices, store information on clients, and create profit and loss and balance sheets by simply clicking a button. This sort of software costs something over £100 for the small business versions, and slightly more if you want the payroll facility, which is useful if you have staff. If you have an accountant or bookkeeper, they may be able to give you some guidance on choosing a programme.

Financial analysis
Whatever system you use to record your income and outgoings, take time each year to do some analysis. Fill in time sheets or make rough estimates as you go along of the time you spend on each project. This can help you work out which clients are most profitable. You will develop a better understanding of where to concentrate your efforts to generate a living income.

Freelance writer Rach Colling says:

> I invoice my clients regularly, either at the end of each project, or the end of each month. Sadly, as a freelance, there's often a bit of a time delay between you doing the work and getting paid for it, but I've been very lucky: everyone has paid up so far. I've been very lucky also that I've been able to spend time building up my clients while doing other things and we haven't had to rely on my income totally. Going freelance is one of those things that you either need the support of a partner to do, or to have a wodge of cash in the bank for those first few months when there's nothing much coming in, I think. I've also tackled accounts using a very simple Excel spread-sheet. Tax returns are rather mind-boggling, but if you do them online they come with good help instructions.

Tax returns
You need to fill in a tax return once a year if you are self-employed. The tax return needs to be sent to the Inland Revenue by the end of October if you submit paper returns and want them to work out how much you owe, or by the end of January if you do your own calculations and submit them online (or have your accountant do this for you). Keep good records, and it can simply be a couple of hours' work to tot up totals and fill in boxes. Speak to a small business adviser from

the Inland Revenue. They can come to your workplace, or home if you work there, and will take time to explain the system to you.

Reducing your tax bill

If you are self-employed you can claim expenses against your tax bill. This means that if you spend several thousand on keeping your business running, this gets taken off your income before it is assessed for tax. You can claim for travel to meet clients, but not to your usual place of work. You can claim for a percentage of utility bills as a home worker: if you work from home, assess what proportion of the space you allocate to work or how much time you spend working. If you are unclear about what you can claim against tax, ask the Inland Revenue adviser or your accountant.

Setting money aside

Don't get caught out spending your earnings straight away. Everything you earn is not profit. Obviously, there will be business bills that you need to pay throughout the year, but you also need to allow money to cover your tax bill. After your first year of trading is completed, sole traders not only have to pay the tax for the year that has passed, but also have to make a payment on account towards the following year's tax. This is based on an estimate of what the tax bill will be. If you have had a good year but don't expect the next year to be as profitable you can negotiate to reduce the advance. If business continues to boom you will still need to pay the tax at the next deadline. You will usually make two separate payments: one on 31 January, and one on 31 July.

VAT

According to the Inland Revenue, 'VAT is a tax on consumer expenditure. It is collected on business transactions, imports and acquisitions.' You may be charged VAT on many essentials you buy for your business. If you register for VAT, you can claim back the VAT you have paid, but, of course, have to add VAT on to your invoices to clients, which, at the time of writing, adds 17.5 per cent to your bills.

As a writer, it is unlikely that you will have to register for VAT from day one. You need to register for VAT if you supply VATable goods and services over a certain value, £67,000 in 2008, and rising by a few thousand each year. It can be beneficial to register voluntarily if you think you will be able to claim back more VAT than you have to pay. This can be the case if you have heavy expenses when starting up.

Once you are registered you need to keep a record of all VAT-rated goods and services you supply and receive. You have to fill in a VAT return with details of your sales and purchases, every few months, online or on a paper form. If the VAT on your sales is more than the VAT on your purchases you pay the difference to the Inland Revenue. You claim VAT back if you have paid more VAT on purchases than you have made on sales.

Where do bookkeepers and accountants come in?
A bookkeeper is a great idea if you are rubbish at record keeping. You can put all your receipts in an envelope, print off bank statements and client bills, and ask the bookkeeper to make them into coherent records. Ideally set up an arrangement where you do this once a month: while a bookkeeper will take a year's worth of receipts and plough through them for you, inevitably you will want this done at the same time of year everyone else does, and end up stressed about completing your tax return on time. A bookkeeper can also help with invoicing, VAT and payroll.

Using an accountant may seem appealing if numbers aren't your strong point, but can take an unattractive chunk out of your income, especially if you have not kept good records. Use a simple spreadsheet or accounts programme such as Quickbooks to keep track of your income and outgoings. If you can't face doing your own tax return you can hand this over to the accountant at the end of the year. Doing it this way helps you know where you stand and keeps the accountant's fees down.

An accountant can be a source of help and advice when you are starting out on a freelance writing career. They can aid you in setting up your finances correctly, advise on whether you want to work as a sole trader or a company, and help you make decisions about whether to register for VAT. You do pay for this advice, but may be able to find free help on some topics from advisers at your local enterprise agency. Have a chat to a couple of local accountants, find out their fees and see what they can offer you, before making a decision.

Local enterprise agencies

An enterprise agency will be available in most areas. The agency is staffed by business advisers who run courses and offer individual appointments. To find the nearest enterprise agency to you, see:

- Business Link, England: www.businesslink.gov.uk, 0845 6009006
- Business Support, Wales: www.business-support-wales. gov.uk, 0300 0603000
- Venture Wales: www.venturewales.com, 0845 0453150
- Highlands and Islands Enterprise, Scotland: www.hie.co.uk, 01463 234171
- Business Gateway, Scotland: www.bgateway.com, 0845 6096611
- Scottish Enterprise: www.scottish-enterprise.com, 0845 6078787 (within Scotland), 0141 228 2000 (from the UK)
- Invest Northern Ireland: www.investni.com, 028 9023 9090.

Contracts

Whenever you agree to do some work with a client, you should have a written contract. An oral agreement, over the phone or face to face is a contract, but you can have difficulty enforcing it if things go wrong. It is much better to have everything in writing. Some companies will want you to sign their contract, while in other cases you can ask clients to agree to your contract.

Creating your own client briefs

If you have to create a contract for some work for a client it need not be complex. You both need to be clear about the work that you have been commissioned to do, and how much you will charge for it. (See the next section for more on setting fees.) Develop a pro forma for client briefs, which lays out key dates and deadlines, and breaks down the different elements in any agreed work. Even if the company or individual requesting the work does not ask for this, emailing over a quick note can clarify any misunderstandings before the work starts. Other things to include in your brief:

- The name and position of person commissioning you.
- A description of the agreed work.
- Deadline(s).
- How the client wants to receive the work: on disc, by email or in print.
- The rights you are licensing, if appropriate.
- The payment and payment terms.

Establish before you start whether the client will reimburse expenses which you incur while doing the job. Find out the terms of payment: will they pay you on delivery of the work or, in the case of magazines, on publication? You may be able to set your own terms and ask for payment within thirty days of the date of the invoice, for example. Make sure you know how the client wants to be invoiced.

A. Writer
47 Anystreet
Yourtown

12 April 2009

Client: John Smith, Editor, Mega Media

Job description: To interview four case studies and write up a case study on each of 500 words. For single use in client magazine and on website for 3 months.

Job cost: £400 per thousand words

Delivery date: 12 May 2009

Rach Colling advises:

Listen to what the client thinks they're after – and then don't be afraid to quiz them. What's their target audience? What are they really trying to do? Have they seen something else that they'd like to emulate? All this will give you some good background when you start to sit down to write, and should help minimize the chances of having to do a complete rewrite later.

You will find getting advice from a solicitor about setting up some basic terms and conditions can be invaluable. Advice in this book can only be a general guideline, and getting a standard contract set up correctly in the first place can save you time and money later on.

J. Freelance
PR Services
Boomtown

Jane Owner
Director
PR Agency
Big Town

1 September 2010

Dear Jane,

Re: Freelance PR Work

I'd just like to confirm that you would like me to work in your office on the 10th, 11th and 12th of September, on the product launch. We have agreed a rate of £300 per day for three days.

Yours sincerely

J. Freelance

Signing a client's contract

Some clients may have a contract that they ask all their suppliers to sign. Read it carefully. Check whether the client is asking you to indemnify them against legal action. You should, of course, take all necessary care to do the work correctly but you may be able to ask for this clause to be removed, or simply score through it before signing. You should check your professional indemnity insurance to make sure that you are covered in case of legal action. If you are unsure about terms in a contract, you may be able to get free advice if you are a member of a professional body such as the NUJ or Society of Authors.

Preventing problems

When you are setting up a project, and as you do the work, keep everything well documented. Make notes of meetings and telephone conversations and retain records of research, drafts and notes. Develop a filing system, which can be as simple as keeping work for each client or project in a box file, so that you can find relevant details if a query arises. Consider how you will store work, as queries can come up even after several years.

Setting fees

One of the hardest things to establish when starting out is how much to charge. It is easy to fall into the trap of undercharging, either through a lack of confidence, or through a lack of appreciation of exactly what your fee has to cover.

If you are self-employed, you have to cover a range of expenses that can soon eat away at what seemed a decent fee. An employer will cover National Insurance contributions, pension payments, office costs, holiday pay, training, recruitment and sick pay for its staff. When you are working for yourself, you need to allow for:

- meetings and travel;
- an appropriate number of drafts, if you are providing work

for the client to agree;
- meeting preparation;
- research;
- background reading;
- administration and accounts.

In more general terms you also need to cover the cost of marketing your business, your premises, utilities, stationery and much more. Remember, when doing your calculations, that you are unlikely to have paid work for forty hours a week, fifty-two weeks a year. Make an allowance for the times when you are doing your own business admin, or even taking a holiday.

Louisa Bird of the Women's Marketing Forum has some tips on pricing:

> Don't be tempted to compete solely on price. When you're starting out especially, it can be tempting to think that if you beat your closest competitors on price, then you'll be the one winning all the clients. Unfortunately, more often than not, the customers you will attract by using this tactic will be the ones that are concerned only with price, and they will be the first ones to stop using your services when they find somebody cheaper (and there will always be somebody cheaper than you). What's worse is that it sets up a negative impression of you and your service and – quite literally – brands you as 'cheap and cheerful', but not necessarily someone to be taken seriously as a long-term service partner.
>
> Consider offering a premium service, at a premium price. It's normally far easier to make a profit with a few high-paying clients than with a larger number of customers who pay you less. What's more, you are likely to have to put roughly the same amount of effort into gaining the less profitable clients as into gaining the high-paying ones, meaning you're losing out on two counts. So avoid discounting wherever possible, and add value instead. Offer a 'Rolls-Royce' service for a 'Rolls-Royce' price – there are always clients out there who are prepared to pay extra for a better quality of service. Sometimes it just takes a little extra confidence and patience to find them.

Market research

If you are setting up a writing business, you will benefit from doing some market research. Look at competitors and see what they are charging. This can be taken into account, along with your own costs, when setting your rates. This sort of research can help you become clear in your own head about the amount you need to charge. It can help if you have some standard rates, per thousand words for copywriting, say, or the amount you need to earn each day or hour. You need to build some flexibility into this. A pharmaceutical company will pay more than a charity. You may want to offer better rates to reliable customers who want work every month, or who pass larger pieces of work your way. You also need to assess the benefit to a client of the work you are doing, and perhaps charge a premium for those clients who demand an urgent piece of copy in a very short time. If you are a journalist, an exclusive with a celebrity is worth far more than another feature, but it can feel difficult to estimate how much.

If you are looking for information on rates, other freelancers are unlikely to share their rates openly, and clients obviously have an interest in how much they pay you. There is a great resource, the NUJ 'Rate for the Job' database, which can give you access to the sort of data you need to get a feel for fees. Journalists submit the amount they were paid, who the work was for and when they did it, and the data is added to the resource, which can be found online at http://media.gn.apc.org/rates/. The information is not just of use to journalists, as it covers rates for PR, books, photography and broadcasting. There are details for prices per thousand words and shifts. The NUJ is clear that this is a survey, not a recommendation, and advises users to check the dates next to a fee, and allow for inflation. It also advises that you do not start negotiations by quoting information from the survey. Instead, you should be aiming to achieve one and a third times the current price.

Another useful resource is Andrew Bibby's Freelance Ready Reckoner, www.andrewbibby.com/reckoner.html, which helps you work out the freelance day rates for equivalent annual gross salaries for employees. It is updated annually. You can also look in the relevant trade media, such as *Campaign, Marketing Week, PR Week*, and the *Guardian* newspaper on Saturdays and Mondays to see ad agency and PR consultancy advertisements for freelancers.

Negotiating

Whenever you pitch for a job there will be a certain amount of negotiation: if the client agrees the price straight away you may worry that you have pitched your price too low. One way round this is to ask the client to name a price first. If you are a negotiation novice, watch others as they do it, and read up on the subject. Write down the plus points of what you have to offer, and identify which parts of your pitch will appeal to the individual you are negotiating with. Play it cool, and don't be afraid to pause, whether you are on the phone or face to face, as this can sometimes encourage the other person to up their offer. Do not appear desperate for the work, even if you are.

Price increases

It pays to review your pricing every year. You may no longer get the annual salary increase you had with an employer, but the price of living will continue to rise. With long-term clients especially, you may want to get into the habit of an annual fee review in January or April. Some may balk at any change, but if you don't ask, you are unlikely to get a better rate.

Deposits

If you are doing some copywriting or PR for a client, you may want to ask for an up-front deposit. You could make this practice for every client, or ask new clients only, or ask for money up front when you know that you will have to make significant outlay to complete the job.

Getting paid on time

Once you have negotiated a rate, be clear about when you expect to be paid. Set this into the contract. Some businesses will have their own protocols. Don't agree to work hoping for payment on delivery and then find you have signed up to be paid ninety days in arrears. In magazines and newspapers, payment may be on publication. If you are a journalist, watch out for 'kill fees', where you get offered only half your original fee if the publication doesn't use your piece. As long as you delivered what you agreed in the contract, hold out for the full fee: often simply by saying that a kill fee is not acceptable you will get the whole fee as agreed.

Submit an invoice when you deliver your work, together with details of the payment terms. You could use a phrase like 'due on receipt' to indicate you want payment immediately, or ask for payment 'within thirty days' or by a certain date. If payment doesn't appear by the specified date, call the accounts department.

Example invoice:

Client: Max Mogul
       Simply Media
       Main Street
       London
       SW1 4DJ
       020 7220 2391

Mike Writer
4 Street
The Suburbs
Greater London
TW17 4NM
020 8385 7976
mike@writingbiz.co.uk

Invoice date: 15 April

Date	Description of work done	Rate ex VAT	Total
27 March	Copy for advertisements 2 days	£450 /day	£900
3 April	Further revisions ½ day	£450 /day	£225
		Subtotal VAT@15% Total	£1,125 £168.75 £1293.75

Payment terms: Payment due no later than thirty days from date of invoice.

Help getting paid

In an ideal world, you would submit your invoice, the client would receive it and immediately issue a cheque or make a transfer. However, life does not work like that. In business, most companies are carefully managing income and outgoings, and some make a point of paying bills at the last possible moment. Some small businesses have someone in to pay bills and do the books for a day each week or month, and if you have missed their day, you have to wait. Others are simply inefficient, and nothing can allow for the invoice that slips off a client's desk. All this means two things. First, you need to plan your cashflow carefully. Working for yourself does not have the security of a regular paycheque, and the way you manage your invoicing and the payment of your own bills can mean the difference between success and failure. Second, you need to develop a system to monitor money due to you, or use accounts software as mentioned above, and have a regular day for chasing up late payments. If you loathe this side of things consider taking on a virtual assistant or bookkeeper to spend a few hours each month issuing invoices and chasing unpaid ones. It can be well worth their fee just to keep your income coming in.

Late payments

However good your systems, there will be clients who pay late, or do not appear to be about to pay up at all. Since 1998, businesses have a statutory right to claim interest from other businesses for the late payment of commercial debt. You can charge interest on late payments at a set rate, and reasonable debt recovery costs. Visit the website of the Better Payment Practice Campaign, www.payontime.co.uk, for more detail on good payment, managing customer credit, and current rates of interest which can be applied to late payments.

If you have to chase a late payment, the simplest thing may be to give the client, or their accounts department, a call. If could be that the invoice has gone astray and they will pay up as soon as you resend it. If the client tells you there are difficulties paying, you will at least be aware of this, and could discuss paying in instalments. If the money does not appear you may want to put your request in writing, giving a date by which you want the money.

If this does not produce the required payment, you could consider getting a solicitor to chase payment. You could use a local solicitor, or a solicitor with a specific debt-chasing service. Thomas Higgins, for example, will send a 'letter before action' for a couple of pounds (www.thomashiggins.com). If you are a member of a union like the NUJ, ask your union for help. It will help if you can show the contract and invoice, and any records of phone calls or letters you have sent to chase the debt. If the letter does not result in payment you can then take your client to court. Again, you can get advice on this from a solicitor. Make the most of legal support from your union or become a member of an organization like the Federation of Small Businesses which has a legal helpline.

Before you set off on this course of action, you need to weigh up the worth of the client. If the client gives you regular work, will you risk losing them if you send a solicitor's letter to chase a debt? Generally, however good a client has been in the past, if they stop paying up, they cease to be a good client.

Tracey 'Word Doctor' Dooley is a creative consultant and business writer. She enjoys writing for a living, but, like many writers, does not enjoy the administrative side of business quite as much. She says:

> Really, I'm not too good at this side of running a business. I ask for a proportion of my fee up front, sometimes the entire amount, before I start a job. This is for three main reasons: (i) I got fed up with being burned by clients, (ii) it shows that a prospect is serious about working with me, and (iii) it is about taking my time and my client's needs seriously. I pay my supplier bills as soon as I can, as a courtesy. I don't usually wait for the thirty-plus days to pass.
>
> It's not all good, though: I am shamefully lacking when it comes to accounting. I tend to do it in one big chunk in January. It means I can carry on chomping my way through a few kilos of chocolates after the festive season.

Tracey's business, MediaMinister.co.uk, specializes in helping clients maximize their results from sales and marketing, so she has some great tips to help new writers grow their businesses:

> I'd say, first and foremost, be patient. Think acorns and big trees and all that. I would certainly talk to those already established in your chosen industry. You can't spend too much time or energy when it comes to assessing in which field or industry your skills and experience would be most useful. So be sure to thoroughly evaluate your business idea, its viability, its originality, the skills or training needed and whether you could successfully carve a niche with it. Then completely research your target market and the expectations of your potential customers in relation to your product or service. Furthermore, you can never go wrong by joining a good business-oriented forum. And be sure to contact your local Business Link or the Federation of Small Businesses for support. Plus, I'd learn how to network more effectively. Also, market vigorously. In fact, don't ever stop. Nor stop asking questions. Perhaps the biggest tip is to never forget that your greatest assets are your current customers. Treat them well. Nurture them. And never neglect them.

Chapter 4

Finding clients

One key issue for any professional writer is to ensure a steady flow of work. This chapter will focus on some of the many ways to find clients, and keep them coming back. In Chapter 2, we looked at your portfolio. To recap, you should set up a file of clippings, and have scanned versions available too. Be ready to send out examples of your work to enquirers and potential clients. This chapter will look at how to start generating those enquiries, and how to turn them into business.

Every writer wanting to earn a living has to start somewhere. Some start by relying entirely on their freelance earnings, but many others start with a mixture of paid employment and freelance work. Some people run their freelance work in the evenings for quite some time alongside a day job. Before I handed in my notice I made some pitches and had some articles accepted, which gave me the confidence to make the move. Look at your outgoings, and work out a way to ensure you can still pay the bills. It is fine to do some self-employed work and still be employed at the same time, but do remember to notify the Inland Revenue of the self-employed work within three months of starting.

Marketing yourself

If you have qualms about this part of writing to earn your living, you are not alone. Few professional writers start out packed with confidence in their own skills, and many are unsure how to promote themselves. It can help if you take a step back: don't look at promoting yourself as a person, and instead look at promoting yourself as a business.

Work out what is great about your writing business. In the previous chapters you should have looked at your skills and knowledge. Note down a few skills you have, or say them out loud, as if you are telling someone else about what you do. Think about the problems you could solve for the businesses you are targeting. Picture the business owner, sitting at their computer, trying to come up with wording for an advertisement or brochure, and describe how your business could help them. Think about ways that your business can help when other businesses might not be able to. What is unique about what you offer?

Take some time to develop a shortlist of the good things about your business – your unique selling points. It is worth putting plenty of effort in at this stage, as you are developing the basis for marketing your business. Pare down your list into a few essential words to describe what you offer. This could become your strap line. Try it out on friends or colleagues, and see if they think it sums up what you want to offer. You might want to have a logo to run alongside your strap line too. And, of course, do you want a name for the business? You may just want to work as Jane Smith, Copywriter, but there can be advantages to having a business name. You may want to take on a business partner at some point, or employ people. A name other than your own can make the business sound bigger too. It can also make it easier to step away from the business if you want to sell your company in a number of years' time

Marketing materials

Once you have a name, logo and strap line, you need to think where you are going to use it. It can be worth investing a little in some promotional materials, but only if you have planned where you will distribute them. Most businesses will benefit from some professional-looking headed paper. Fortunately, with good quality home printing technology, you do not need to rush and invest several hundred pounds with a local printer to start off. See what you can design on your own computer, or rope in a friend or colleague with graphic design skills. Run off a few sheets of headed paper at a time until you know what sort of volumes you are going to be using. Many commercial writing businesses operate largely online, so you may find investing in boxes of thousands of sheets of headed paper to be a waste of money.

Business cards may be a more worthwhile investment. There is an appreciable difference between the quality of a home-printed card and one which has been done by a professional printer. Take a little time to make the most of your card, and do not follow traditional formats blindly. Look at the size of your card, to start with. Can you get everything you want to convey into a business card, or might you be better off investing in a postcard-sized product? Here are some essentials to include on your card:

- The business name
- Your name
- Your job title
- Mobile *and* landline numbers
- Email
- Website
- Postal address
- What your business offers
- Its unique selling points.

If you are a sole trader, choose a job title that suits you: it is entirely up to you whether you want to be a 'Copywriter' or choose something more general like 'Director' or 'Owner'.

It is vital to remember that a business card has two sides. You may want to leave some space on the back to write a note as you hand a card over. This can encourage the person to whom you have given the card to retain it. However, you can also put in some of the strong selling points for your business. If you are creating a postcard you have even more room for images and logos.

Crumpet Copywriting
www.crumpetcopywriting.co.uk

Snappy solutions to all your copywriting problems

leaflets – brochures – flyers

Crumpet Copywriting
www.crumpetcopywriting.co.uk

Jane Smith, Director

jane@crumpetcopywriting.co.uk
07900 99000   0207 356 789
73 Green Lane, London SW8 1DJ

Leaflets and flyers

You may also want to create a leaflet or flyer, to describe what you offer in more depth. Focus on three or four key services that will appeal to your target audience, and remember to include your unique selling points. Think about whether you want to include your prices. Detailed price lists may give potential clients the confidence to get in touch, but leaflets go out of date if you increase your prices. Illustrate flyers with up-to-date testimonials from satisfied customers. In previous chapters we looked at ways of offering work to charities or swapping skills with other start-up businesses in order to generate some testimonials if you have none.

A professional designer will improve the look of your leaflet, but even if you are starting on a budget you should be able to come up with something acceptable on your computer. Before you get your leaflets printed, think about where you are going to use them. This applies to all marketing materials: only print what you have plans for, with a small margin for extras. Otherwise you will end up with a box of leaflets sitting on your desk, when they should be out there working for you. Look at the costs of doing a leaflet drop to local businesses: can you find a trustworthy teen or local distribution company to put them out for you? Business and enterprise centres are worthwhile places to target as you will cover lots of businesses with one drop off.

Proof it

Make sure that all your materials are error free. Employ a professional proofreader if necessary. (See contact details for the Society for Editors and Proofreaders at the end of the book.) You need your promotion materials to be a positive advertisement for all your writing skills, grammar and spelling included.

Plan your promotion

It is worth making some plans for how you will promote your business over the next twelve months. Use a diary, or set up a document on your computer, and note down ideas in each month. Spend a few hours planning your promotion and you can slot it in when you have a few minutes free. It is vital to keep plugging away at promoting your business, even when you are busy, to keep your profile high and work flowing steadily. Put in slots each month for distributing your marketing materials, and remember to go back and top them up if necessary. Think about advertisements, face-to-face promotion and networking, making the most of niches and angles, and online promotion. Add in new ideas as they occur to you, and go through the plan properly every few months. Read on to get more idea of how these can help your business.

Advertisements

While we are talking about marketing tools, it is worth thinking about advertising. Approach advertising strategically, as it can help build your business. However, do not rely on a single advert to bring in all the clients you need. Advertisements work best as part of an overall plan, and can be a costly waste of money on their own. Be clear about what your potential clients read, and target the right publications. Ask for a magazine's media pack to find out more about their readers. It can be worth taking a long shot with small local publications like parish magazines. Prices can be low and people may like to use a local service.

You can also get a copy of the publication's rate card, which gives you a top line for the price of an advert. It is always worth asking for a discount. Call near to the deadline for the publication, and, if you have your advertisement ready, you may be able to snap up a last-minute space at a good price. You can also get discounts for booking a series of advertisements: it can, however, be hard to tell in advance if an ad is going to work well for you.

You may be lucky and find the perfect publication for you: if you are working in a specialist area and are the only copywriter advertising in a trade publication you could find it a good source of business. However, many small businesses find advertising to be a costly investment with a poor return.

Directory listings

Perhaps more effective, and certainly more focused than much advertising, are directories of freelance journalists. These list your details so editors or clients can search and find the people they need. All the directories listed below rank well on Google at time of writing, which is important as more and more people are searching online to find writers.

People4business.com

For all types of freelancers, but with a large media section. Allows you to set your rate, which leads to an enormous variety of rates per hour. Clients can give ratings for freelancers they have used.

Free listings for freelancers, 10 per cent fee for clients making a booking through the service.

The NUJ Freelance Directory (http://www.freelancedirectory.org/)
Covers writers, editors, sub-editors, broadcasters, scriptwriters, web designers, translators, trainers and researchers in UK and Ireland. Available in print and online, arranged by region, skill and specialism. Entry is for NUJ members. You can choose between a basic entry and an enhanced one for a small fee of £10 or £20 which means you remain in the directory for two years.

Journalism.co.uk
For a slightly larger fee of £50 you can be listed in this directory for one year, which includes a freelance bulletin board and email address. The directory is searchable by name, skill, specialism and location. Includes your picture and links to your work, website or blog and email. Featured on home page on rotation. Has the advantage of being a site used for advertising journalism positions, and hence visited by employers.

Daryl Wilcox Publishing Freelancer Directory
(www.journalistdirectory.com)
Currently free for journalists. You can specify your specialisms and areas of work, upload detailed profile information and also opt to receive relevant press releases.

Freelance UK (www.freelanceuk.com)
Currently free to join. As with other directories, you can specify your areas of work and web address. You can also upload a document about what you offer.

Press Gazette Freelancer Directory (www.pressgazette.co.uk)
For £50, you get a twelve-month listing in the magazine and a twelve-month listing online under a heading of your choosing.

CiB (www.cib.uk.com/contents/freelancers)
The British Association of Communicators in Business (CiB) also

has a small database of members available for freelance work. Clients ask for a job to be mailed round to members.

Face-to-face promotion
One of the most effective ways of getting work is through people you meet. You may get started with work for a friend of a friend, and word of mouth is one of the strongest recommendations for a business. It is therefore important to maximize these opportunities, and look for ways to meet people who may want to commission you to write for their business.

Word of mouth
Make it easy for happy clients to refer you to colleagues. Give out a small supply of business cards to each client, and ask them to pass them on. Do not be afraid of asking for recommendations: most people who have liked what you have done will be only too glad to help you. You may want to give incentives to encourage referrals. This is not as simple as operating a reward card, but think about whether you give a client who is a good referrer a discount on future work, or a small gift.

Networking
More and more small-business owners are getting into networking, a structured way of meeting business owners and people in a position to give you work. Media life coach Joanne Mallon says, 'Never stop networking. The media industry runs on contacts much more than official job ads. Don't stay on the outside, moaning that you don't have the right contacts. Think about what you need to do to create more contacts – whether through your current connections or by meeting new people.'

There are plenty of traditional business networks, such as local chambers of commerce. You pay an annual fee and get to attend meetings over breakfast, lunch or dinner. Choose a group that meets at a time that suits you. There are also women-only groups, and other groups in specialist sectors. A face-to-face networking group like this usually gives you the chance to do a short pitch for your business, and give and accept referrals from other members.

You can probably attend for one or two meetings to see what the group is like before deciding to join. Some groups are strict about attendance, and require that you send a substitute or limit your absences. Others have targets for referrals, so check out the rules and make sure you can stick to them.

There are many networking groups for writers, with a mixture of online networking (see below) and meetings including:

- Media Women, www.mediawomenuk.com
- Journobiz, www.journobiz.com
- Schmooze and Booze www.schmoozeandbooze.com
- Women in Journalism www.womeninjournalism.co.uk

Cold and warm calling
You may make some contacts through networking that you want to follow up, or you may want to go in cold and target some new companies in your area. To do this successfully, do some research first. Start by picking the businesses that you target carefully. Aim for small companies who do PR in-house or medium-sized firms that don't hire big ad agencies. Estate agents or web development companies may need copywriters. Look at your local business directory or high street for more ideas, or follow up some types of business from this list:

- Advertising agencies
- Business owners
- Direct marketing specialists
- Graphic design agencies
- Individuals
- Internet businesses
- Local businesses
- Marcomms (marketing communications) agencies
- Marketing and communications managers
- PR consultancies
- Professional bodies
- Publishing houses
- Quangos

If you want to work for a government department, there may be procurement processes which you need to go through. Large companies may also have requirements for contractors.

Once you have a shortlist of target companies, find out about each one. Assess where you might be able to contribute, and call to find out who is responsible for commissioning this sort of work. It can be easier in a small company, but may require some persistence to get the right person in a larger one. Have a chat on the phone. Outline what you offer, and ask them open questions about the sort of writing work that they contract out. Think about your aim for the phone call: do you want to arrange a meeting so you can show them some of your work, or would you rather the outcome be that you send in some examples? Make sure you book a follow-up call if you are sending in examples of work. If you arrange a meeting, bring in copies of your work that you can leave along with a business card.

Niche marketing
When you are marketing your commercial writing business it can help to develop a niche. If, for example, you are well informed about health and complementary therapies, you might want to focus on working for companies in that field. You can use your knowledge and experience to demonstrate how you can get up to speed quickly with complex materials using technical language, for example. Louisa Bird of the Women's Marketing Forum advises, 'Specialize as much as possible. If you used to be an estate agent, consider writing about property. Find a niche based on your own experience.'

Your reputation
Once you have focused on a niche for your work, it is worth building your reputation in this area. Are there trade publications or websites where you could contribute an article or some tips? Keep them informed about your relevant business news and new services that you offer. Aim to be seen as an expert in your field, as this will help potential clients develop trust and confidence in your skills. If you get any media coverage, add this to your website, and use extracts in your flyers. A journalist's opinion on your business

can have more weight than anything you write yourself. Always ask permission before using quotes and extracts.

Online networking and promotion

Networking can take place both face to face and online. Try to use both routes, as you can otherwise miss out on potential business.

Online basics
Before you start networking online, make sure you have an online presence which showcases your services and talents well. In Chapter 2 we looked briefly at the first steps involved in setting up a website. Now, read on to find out about how your website can be used to promote your writing and get you new clients.

Louisa Bird of the Women's Marketing Forum says:

> Websites are an indispensable promotional tool, especially if you are a freelancer working from home. Quite a few people are nervous about creating their own website, but there are plenty of low-cost options that you can customize yourself without it looking like something created by your fourteen-year-old son.

Make your site sell
Good, clear, concise content for your website is a great advertisement for your own copywriting skills. Remember that copywriting for the web is not the same as writing for print. Content needs to be easy to read at a glance. Use fewer words and shorter page lengths than if you were writing for a print publication. Break long sentences into shorter ones, and use bullets and numbered lists. Avoid jargon, take out long words, and replace them with short ones.

What do you want your readers to do?
One of the most important things to remember is to have a clear aim for your website. For most writers, the aim is to get clients to use their services. What outcomes do you want from the website?

If you are setting up a commercial writing business, you want visitors to the site to find out about your services, become confident that you offer what they need, and then get in touch with you. Focus on these aims and outcomes as you write the page content. On each page, give the reader the means to learn about your services, develop confidence in your skills and experience, and contact you.

Search-engine optimization

As well as making your site clear and accessible for human visitors, you also need to make sure that it is going to be picked up by search engines. This is an essential part of developing a successful website, one which helps you to promote your business. If your site ranks well in search engines, clients will be able to find you easily. The main search engine to focus on is Google, which is responsible for the vast majority of searches in the UK.

Hidden factors

Behind every website is HTML code, which prescribes how the website appears. The code will also include metatags, the key words that are relevant to each page within your website. The most important metatag is the title. Think carefully about the essential words to describe each page. Search engines may use the title metatag as the listing title. Then, explain a little more about the page in the description tag, which will be displayed beneath the listing title if your site appears as the result of a search.

Choosing keywords

What would you type into a search engine if you were looking for a copywriter, a public relations freelancer or someone who could edit a company brochure? As a writer you should be well placed to come up with a range of words to describe what you do. Make a list, and run some internet searches yourself to see what you come up with. Visit Google's keyword tool and type in your keywords to generate a list of further words and combinations of words you can use. Use your final list of words both in the metatags and in the text that the reader views. Don't overuse your keywords: you still need to make sure that the text flows well.

What are you selling?
Whether you are using a blog (see below and Chapter 10) or getting a designer to create your website, the most important thing is the content. Focus on what problem you are solving for clients, and use the words on your site to sell your solution to them. Before you start putting anything online, work out how many pages you want to have on your website, and the purpose of each. Most writers' sites will need the following:

- Home page
- Skills and experience
- Services
- Menu
- Contact details
- Legal details
- Links.

Home page
Use the home page to entice people into your site, with a broad outline of what you offer and links to take readers more deeply in. Work out the pathways people will need to follow to find out about your services, for example, and make sure they can get to the information in just two or three clicks.

Skills and experience
Most serious potential clients will want to look into your background before they employ you. This is the place for your online portfolio. Rather than simply sticking up a CV, pull out the key skills you offer, and describe them. Back this up with evidence to show how and when you have used the skills. As a writer, this is the place to put links to your work. You could link to websites you have written the copy for, or have short extracts from articles you have written, with the option to click to read the whole thing. If you have contributed the copy for brochures or leaflets, ask clients if it is

possible to use the item on your website. This is an advertisement for their service too, and will demonstrate your skills in action. If you can, add in client comments about your work.

Services

Be clear about the services you can offer. Clients may not be sure what they want, and the clearer you are, the more likely they are to identify how you can help them. Give examples of the sort of writing you do, including copywriting, editing, writing for newsletters or websites, for example. You may want a separate page for each service. On each page you could describe what you offer, and include case studies of how other businesses have used your services. Again, testimonials from clients can give potential customers confidence. If you ask for feedback on every job you complete, and add comments to your website each time, you will build up a good range of independent opinions on your work, with the added benefit of new content for your site which will help your site feature well on search-engine results.

Menu

Think about how people will enter your site. A few may come in through the front page, but what about those who search on, say, copywriting, and go straight to your copywriting page? Will the information on there still make sense? Is there a clearly visible menu in a sidebar, or at the top or bottom of the page, so they can easily navigate the site and find other relevant pages?

Contacts

Think about how people can get in touch with you. I'd advise having a mobile number and email address available to view on every page. You are required to have a physical address, not a PO box, somewhere on your website. If you have an office, you may want to put this on the contacts page, together with a map to help visitors find you. If you work from home, you may want to put your address somewhere less obvious, such as in your terms and conditions.

Legal details

It is good practice to have terms and conditions available on your website. You should cover how you deal with complaints, and how you keep clients' data securely. If customers can purchase your services online there are legal requirements, the Distance Selling Regulations, which you must comply with. If you operate as a registered company, you need to display your company number and the registered office address.

Links

Your links page is a way to point clients towards other, complementary services and useful resources. Build good links with companies where clients also require copywriting, and you can make referrals to each other. You might want to link up with a web designer a graphic designer, or a printing business, for example. Take a measured approach to link swapping. This used to be seen as a way to get your site rated more highly by search engines, but large numbers of mutual links do not help with this. It is better to have a few carefully selected and relevant links, and then include more links in new content as you add it. This works particularly well for blog entries, for example.

Other pages

There are plenty of other possible pages you can add to your site. You may want to have a 'frequently asked questions' page. A page outlining details of the media coverage you have had for your business is a good advertisement, especially if you are working in PR. Think about having a place where visitors can sign up for email updates and newsletters.

Updating your site

Don't make your site a static entity. Add new content on a regular basis. This has the dual benefit of enticing visitors back and getting search engines to rank your site more highly. The need to add content regularly may inform how you choose to create the site. If you get a designer to create it for you, make sure there is a simple way for you to add content yourself.

Blogging

Blogging is both a way to update your site and a good promotion tool. Plus, as a writer, you will probably enjoy having somewhere to put down your thoughts on a regular basis. You can use software from a publishing platform like Wordpress, either hosted on and integrated into your own website, or hosted by the publisher. Blog regularly, and link to other blogs which you like. Make comments on other people's blogs, and invite comments on your own. Becoming part of the network of bloggers will get your writing in front of a wider audience, and can even lead to business (see Chapter 10).

Newsletters

A regular newsletter is a great way to keep clients up to date with the services that you offer and encourage new business. It can also act as a showcase for your writing skills. Have a sign-up box on your website, and get permission from each new client to add their name to your mailing list. Aim to send out a newsletter every fortnight, month or quarter: pick a frequency that you can maintain. You may want to add news from clients, and interesting information you have come across which is relevant to your business and that of your readers. You may want to take a short piece from your blog and work it up into an article for your newsletter. This, in turn, could be added to your website to provide fresh and interesting content for visitors.

Online networks

Now you have your site, you need to start spreading the word about what you offer in the online community. Start by looking at the many business networks there are in the internet. These networks help business people to connect. Some just operate online, while others host face-to-face networking events and seminars too. Ecademy, www.ecademy.com, is one of the biggest and oldest online networks, with thousands of members across the globe and hundreds of smaller clubs and communities. LinkedIn, www.linkedin.com, allows you to set up a personal profile and make business contacts too.

Most networks have some sort of free trial, after which you need to pay a monthly or annual membership fee. Make the most of the trial to see how many business contacts you can build up, and whether you can turn these contacts into contracts for work. It can be hard to measure the benefits of this sort of network: it may take months to build your reputation and develop the trust needed for people to ask you to give them a quote for some copywriting, or you may strike it lucky straight away.

Freelance writer, editor and proofreader Rach Colling explains how she promotes her business:

> I usually try and spend some time every week keeping an eye open for new work – looking at local business news, freelance websites, etc. I tend to work in the areas of higher education or e-business but to be honest I can tackle anything. My clients vary from government bodies to local businesses – it's a nice mixture.

Rach has some advice for new writers:

> Network. Most of my clients have come through people I've previously worked with, or people I have a connection to. Try using LinkedIn, for example, or joining a discussion list like mediawom-enuk. Get your work out there – set up your own website, blog or whatever. But also be prepared to pitch for work – it doesn't hurt to send in an application for anything, even if you wind up not getting it. One day your portfolio will end up on the right table at the right time.

Rach's own website is www.rachcolling.co.uk, with a page about Rach, a page for her portfolio, her blog, contact details and a page of useful links for writers.

Business forums
You might also want to join a business forum. This is a website with the facility for members to post messages on all sorts of business topics. You can get to know other business owners, and ask questions or give advice. The main benefit of joining a forum

is that you will get a chance to ask other business owners for their experiences on accounting matters, IT and the internet and many more relevant topics. It can be like having office colleagues, even if you are working alone. Different forums will have varying rules about promoting your business, so check before you plug your services blatantly. Whatever the rules, you can build your reputation by being a source of good advice on copywriting and content, which will, in the long term, lead to enquiries and business. Look at UK Business Forums, www.ukbusinessforums. co.uk.

BT Tradespace is another online community where it can pay to have a presence. You can opt for a free Tradespace page, which allows you to have information about your business, host your blog and display your services. You can upload images too, making it another place to showcase work you are proud of. You can also link to other businesses. See www.bttradespace.com.

Social networking

There is an indistinct border between online networks used for social purposes and those used to promote businesses. More and more businesses are developing a presence on Facebook, www.facebook.com. You have the opportunity to create a page for your business, and encourage clients to become 'fans'. Perhaps more to the point is to develop your own personal profile, and build links with individuals. Add former colleagues and new networking contacts as Facebook friends, and have details about your business writing services on your profile for them to see.

MySpace, www.myspace.com, and YouTube, www.youtube. com, can also be places to promote your writing business. How useful they are will depend on the sort of clients you are hoping to reach. If you want to work in the music media, many bands have a presence on MySpace. YouTube offers you a place to upload videos. You could create a video of yourself offering professional advice as another way to promote your services and build your reputation.

Making the most of enquiries

So, using your face-to-face and online contacts, you should be starting to get the word out about your writing business. Enquiries may be rolling in, or just trickling, but it is important to treat each and every enquiry seriously, as it could be the start of a long-term business relationship. Here are some tips:

- Acknowledge enquiries promptly. Even if you can't send a full quote, send an email to let the enquirer know when you can send more details.
- Make it personal. Don't fall into the trap of making all your emails sound the same. Clients want to know that there is a person handling their enquiry rather than an autoresponder.
- Ask for more details. Be as clear as you can about what the client wants and when before you give the quote. Don't be embarrassed to ask for in-depth detail: clients will appreciate that you are being thorough.
- Send a quote in writing. It doesn't matter if you email or post a quote for a job: ask the enquirer what they prefer. Do, however, make sure that everything is written down so that there are no misunderstandings.
- Use your portfolio. If sending a quote by post, include an example of something relevant you have done in the past. If emailing, include a link to a piece of work in your online portfolio. This can give a client confidence in your abilities.
- Follow up. If you have sent off a quote, you may want to give the enquirer a quick call the following day to see if they have any more questions to ask. This sort of personal contact can help you build a relationship, and may give you the edge over a competitor. If you can get a booking for a piece of work there and then, great. If not, fix up a time to call back. Do make this call: even if you get a 'no thank you', it is an opportunity to find out where your pitch failed, and improve it for next time.

Agencies

As well as, or instead of, promoting yourself as a freelance writer, you may want to work through an agency. If you're thinking of approaching an agency, Steve Lodge who runs Copywriter UK, www.copywriteruk.co.uk, advises:

> Agencies will often want to see a portfolio, and it's vital to build one that is broad-based and comprehensive. The jury's out on whether a copywriter should be niche or multi-skilled, but it can help to focus a portfolio on your strengths, be they press releases, long copy or creative concepts. Reliability is the key. You have to understand the brief, turn round a competent piece of work, ensure the job is proof-read and with no errors and above all ensure that the turnaround meets the deadline. That's often a big task and one that freelancers fall down on.

PART TWO

Areas of work

This section of the book looks at the different areas where writers can specialize. Developing a niche will help you focus your promotion efforts and build your reputation and business. Read on to find advice on each sector, alongside the experiences of successful business writers.

Chapter 5

Advertising

From Dorothy L. Sayers to Fay Weldon, many writers have chosen advertising as a career. Coming up with advertising copy can use your creativity and enable you to hone your writing skills. If you want a business writing career, and are interested in working in advertising, read on. This chapter looks at the key skills you will need, tells you about how to train, and how and where to get work.

Your personality

Are you full of big ideas? To work in advertising, you need to have lots of imagination and creativity. You will be working as part of a team, and need to be good at communicating with other team members, the client, and ultimately the target audience for your work. On the downside, working in advertising can be competitive. You can end up doing long hours to meet tight deadlines.

The job

Many copywriters are employed, but most agencies will also have a pool of freelance creative teams which they use, comprising an art director and a copywriter. Around 75 per cent of jobs are London based.

Specialization and sectors

Because of the high level of competition, you may find more opportunities if you can develop a niche or specialist knowledge. Unique understanding of a highly technical area can make you indispensable. You could specialize in fast-moving consumer goods (FMCG), advertising brands of food, cleaning products and other products purchased on a regular basis. Alternatively you may be interested in consumer durables, including 'white goods' like fridges and washing machines or 'brown goods' such as TVs and radios. Financial services advertising has specific regulations, and hence requires specialist copywriters who are familiar with these rules. You could find work for a large retail group, such as a supermarket or chain store, for utilities companies or in the travel industry. There is also a sector of advertising dedicated to business-to-business marketing, focusing on specialized professional and trade media.

While you may think advertisements are there to sell a product, there are many other purposes. Your client may be a charity or a government department, which wants to promote a message to change people's behaviour.

If you are thinking of working in advertising, start looking at the advertisements around you. Think about what works well. Assess who each advertisement is appealing to. See if you can find data about who the company was actually targeting, and whether they have released figures on the effect of the advertisement. Think about how the words are used: an advertisement often relies on very few words, combined with a striking image, to catch people's eye and convey a message in a matter of seconds. Read *Campaign* magazine to get an insight into the advertising industry, and check out Brand Republic, the website for advertising, marketing, media and PR.

Writing in advertising

In advertising agencies and departments, copywriters work as part of an advertising team, in partnership with an art director. The copywriter or 'creative' is responsible for the verbal and textual content of the advertisement, while the art director focuses on the look and appeal. You could find yourself writing copy for advertisements ranging from slogans to text for a leaflet, or a script or jingle for radio or TV.

What does a copywriter do?

On a day-to-day basis, you may find yourself juggling several different projects. You will need to create ideas with your art director, and present them to an agency creative director and account team, who will help focus which ideas are to be shown to the client. You will need to be able to explain the thinking behind the words you have used.

The client may make suggestions for changes, or the advertisement may be tested on a focus group, comprising people from the target audience who comment on a number of possible ad campaign variants. You need to be able to take on board this input and adapt your original idea, while still conveying the main message and complying with the relevant code. The ability to constantly revise and rewrite your work is vital.

If you are working on TV or radio ads, you may also be involved in casting actors. You may need to liaise with photographers, designers, production companies and printers.

Find an art director

Copywriters in advertising tend to work in partnership with an art director. If you are going to pitch for a job you'll need someone who can come up with creative artwork. Working as a team, you get the benefit of being able to bounce ideas off each other too. If you are new to the industry it can be hard to find someone to work with so NABS, the advertising industry's benevolent organization, organizes a Lonely Hearts Club in collaboration with The Talent Business. At these sessions twelve to fourteen people get together to share portfolios, chat and swap numbers, with the aim of finding a creative partner. There are also guest speakers from all sectors of the industry who talk about their experiences, answer questions and set briefs for new creative pairs to work on. See www.nabs.org.uk for more information.

Key skills for advertising

To work in advertising, you need to be able to listen to and understand the client's needs. You should get a brief, outlining what the client wants to promote, who they are targeting, and the message they need to get across. You need to be able to come up with a number of original ideas, and work with a team and the client to choose the best one. To see if you can work to a brief, check out some of the examples of real-life creative briefs on the Institute of Practitioners in Advertising (IPA) website, www.ipa.co.uk.

Working to a brief
Start to familiarize yourself with client briefs. From your first piece of advertising work, you will need to be able to understand a brief, spot areas where you need more information, and learn how to liaise with a client and meet their needs as well as come up with creative copy. The brief is the essential basis for any copywriting project, and misunderstandings or lack of clarity at this stage can lead to more rewrites or client dissatisfaction.

What's in a brief?
The ideal brief will tell you where the client, brand or product is now, and where the client wants to get to through the advertisement they have asked you to create. It should define the brand position, and fill you in on the key business issues. A clear focused end point or aim for the project will save both you and the client time and money. It can also make it easier to negotiate the correct rate for the project, although if you are a copywriter working for an agency this is unlikely to be your responsibility.

Briefs vary enormously in complexity, but are rarely long documents. If the agency has worked on a brand for a number of campaigns you will get less detail than for a new brand launch. For any briefing, though, it is important to have objectives laid out, and a number of success criteria, so you and the client can be clear about whether your advertisements have met their requirements. Make sure the objectives are specific rather than vague. Ask what changes to the brand image are desired, and what this will do for the business.

According to *The Client Brief*, a joint industry guideline document based on research with clients and agencies, a good brief should contain the following sections:

1   Project management
2   Where are we now?
3   Where do we want to be?
4   What are we doing to get there?
5   Who do we need to talk to?
6   How will we know we've arrived?
7   Practicalities
8   Approvals.

Depending on the task in hand, each section will contain a varying amount of detail. Any brief needs to take into account the brand's marketing and communications strategy and other programmes that are taking place.

The 'Who do we need to talk to?' section will be all about the target audience. It can include information like their occupation, age range, sex, habits and activities. There may be more than one audience group. To find out more, download a copy of *The Client Brief* from www.ipa.org.uk.

Once you have seen a written brief, it helps enormously to talk things through face to face with the client. A verbal briefing will allow you to pull out any inconsistencies, pick up anything that has been overlooked, and clarify exactly what the client wants.

Depending on the sector you work in, you may need to understand technical documents and paraphrase them for a non-technical audience. Whatever area you work in, you will occasionally get jobs which go outside your expertise, so it is essential to be able to take in new information speedily, and understand it. The ability to write in the language of your target audience is also important, and you need to be able to switch from one writing style for one project to another for a different audience in a matter of minutes.

Writing style

You need to be creative with words to work in advertising, and have plenty of resources in order to get a message across in a few words. Writing to a particular length is a skill that needs to be practised: it can be harder if you need to keep your message to a handful of words than if you have to write several thousand. Everything you write needs to be clear and persuasive. As with all writing jobs, good proofreading skills are essential. You need to be familiar with a thesaurus and dictionary, and able to check facts, grammar and spelling.

Creativity

Advertising is 'all about talent' according to Ann Murray-Chatterton of the IPA, which is good news if you are full of ideas and trying to get into advertising. Ann continues, 'A copy test doesn't assess your writing skills, but looks at whether you can come up with ideas. We're not looking for beautifully crafted copy at this stage.' Ann suggests signing up for the IPA Diagonal Thinking self-assessment. This is an online test to help you see if you have the ability to think in two complementary ways, with your brain oscillating between linear or rational thinking and creative or lateral thinking. This has been shown to be an important skill for advertising.

What you need to know

When working in advertising, you need to be very clear about the codes of advertising practice, and make sure that what you write meets the rules. The main principles of the advertising standards codes are that ads should not mislead, cause harm or offend. The

Committee of Advertising Practice (CAP) governs the British Code of Advertising, Sales Promotion and Direct Marketing. This is the rule book for non-broadcast advertisements, sales promotions and direct marketing communications. Broadly, you need to be sure that advertisements are legal, decent, honest and truthful, but the code runs to nearly forty pages, with separate regulations for advertising to children and for environmental, health and beauty claims, amongst other areas.

The Advertising Standards Authority (ASA) is the independent body that endorses and administers the Code, as well as the Radio Advertising Standards Code and the TV Advertising Standards Code. Again, there are specific rules for the advertising of different products, from medicines to motor vehicles to firearms, and for price claims and VAT, testimonials, guarantees and the use of the word 'free'.

Anyone can complain to the ASA, and the body also monitors advertisements itself. If it finds an advert which breaches a code, it will approach the advertiser; most will agree to make the required change or remove the advertisement altogether. The Office of Fair Trading and Ofcom are called in if changes are not made.

If you are creating an advertisement, you can run it by an advisory body to ensure it meets their requirements. Clearcast checks ads on behalf of TV broadcasters before they go on air, the Radio Advertising Clearance Centre checks national radio ads and the CAP Copy Advice team provides a pre-publication advice service for advertisements in other media.

You can find the codes at www.asa.org.uk/asa/codes/.

Target audiences

As with many types of writing, it is important to have a good understanding of who the advertisement is for – your target audience. You may build up a specialist area, and work on advertisements to business or advertisements to consumers. A consumer audience will be described by its age range, sex, region, behaviours and lifestyle. Alternatively, you may be devising an advertisement to target small, medium or large businesses, or businesses categorized by their type of activity, or even a particular decision-maker within companies, such as the IT director or those working in Human Resources (HR).

The media
When working in advertising, you need to have a good working knowledge of the media. Look at BRAD (British Rate and Data) for details and information about the media, explore websites belonging to publications or those which offer overviews of the industry, like MediaUK, www.mediauk.com. BRAD may be available in reference libraries.

Posters
Poster advertising is probably one of the first things you think about when asked about adverts. Contractors own or lease sites, and sell space to advertisers for fixed periods. Some posters are outdoors, others are in places like tube and train stations. You can work on static displays or have to contend with moving ads which allow three ads to be displayed in the space of one. Digital displays are becoming more common and require somewhat different content.

Print media: newspapers – national dailies, regional daily and evening, local free and paid for
National daily newspapers break down into broadsheet or 'serious' publications, such as the *The Times*, *Telegraph* and *Guardian*, mid-range tabloids like the *Mail* and *Express*, and popular tabloids like the *Sun*, *Star* and *Mirror*. Each different publication will have its own reader demographics. Newspapers run display advertising as well as classifieds, the small text adverts listed by section, usually in the back of the publication. Advertising plays a major role in a newspaper's finances.

Print media: magazines
Magazines can be categorized into a number of sectors, the largest of which is the national women's weeklies and monthlies. There is a smaller number of men's magazines. If you start examining magazines in a big store like Borders, for example, you will be

surprised at the enormous number of specialist consumer magazines. There is also a vast quantity of professional, industry, retail, trade and technical magazines. Many companies produce their own magazine, or have it created for them by a contract publisher (see Chapter 6).

More about print media

To find out more about how print media is structured in the UK and keep up with the latest news, visit the website of the Periodical Publishers' Association, the association for publishers and providers of consumer, customer and business media in the UK at www.ppa.co.uk and the Newspaper Society, the voice of Britain's regional and local press at www.newspapersoc.org.uk.

Radio

Commercial radio accounts for more than half of the UK's listening. There are more than 200 stations, with enormous scope for advertising.

Commercial television

Commercial television breaks down into:

- terrestrial (the ITV group of regional companies, Channel 4)
- satellite (BSkyB, CNN, MTV)
- cable
- digital.

Again, there has been enormous growth in the last twenty years, with an exponential increase in the number of channels available. The possibility for advertising has grown at a similar pace, offering smaller companies the chance to afford advertising on a more minor or specialist and appropriate channel to reach the audience they want.

Cinema

Cinema is useful for attracting a younger audience. Two companies sell advertising time in cinemas, Pearl & Dean and Carlton

Screen Advertising.

Direct mail and telephone marketing
Royal Mail is the main player in the direct marketing field. Telemarketing covers receiving calls as a response to direct response advertising as well as outbound cold calling.

Qualifications

You do not have to have a particular qualification to work in advertising, but, given the level of competition, you will find any qualification an advantage. Useful degree subjects include journalism, English, media studies and marketing.

You could look for a postgraduate diploma or master's in advertising, which is offered by a number of universities in the UK. Check out Kingston University, Falmouth College of Arts, Buckinghamshire New University, Bournemouth University, Napier University and the University of Leeds, among others.

Alternatively, take the Communication, Advertising and Marketing Education Foundation Diploma in Marketing Communications which comprises four thirty-hour modules in Public Relations, Direct Marketing and Sales Promotion, Advertising and Integrated Media, and one sixty-hour module in Marketing and Consumer Behaviour. The diploma can be studied intensively over a series of weekends, by distance learning, full or part time.

Experience

Advertising can be a competitive area to try to get into, but as Ann Murray-Chatterton says, the industry is experiencing 'a dearth of good copywriters', so if you can get noticed you may have a chance.

If approaching agencies, you should have a portfolio of work or 'book' to show them. Full of examples of ads you have worked on, this should highlight your creativity as well as showcasing your writing ability and the different styles you can use. Ann Murray-Chatterton says, 'When a creative director sees your portfolio they will be looking for signs of creative brilliance'. D&AD – the Design and Art Directors' Association – runs workshops to help you build an advertising portfolio and make industry contacts – see www.dandad.org or call 020 7840 1111. NABS offers Portfolio Crit sessions, where you get advice from a senior creative on how to make your portfolio more relevant, carefully planned and well structured so it stands out from others. Find out more about the service at www.nabs.org.uk or call the NABS consultancy team on 0845 602 4497

Experience counts, so if you have not worked in advertising before, try to arrange a placement with an agency. There is a list of agencies that offer work experience on the Institute of Practitioners in Advertising website. Both the IPA and educational charity D&AD run graduate placement schemes. You could also look for work experience in a marketing company. If you work in a large company that has an advertising department, see if you can arrange some experience there. Work experience placements will help you make some contacts and develop your portfolio. NABS has lots of resources to help you if you want to get into advertising. It offers career management consultancy and mentoring.

Nigel Fletcher started thinking about working in advertising while studying for an MA in Creative Writing from the University of East Anglia. He says:

> In hindsight, I think the main benefit for an advertising writer in taking an academic degree is that it helps to discipline the thinking process which is useful for working out the marketing side of things. The creative bit you have to add yourself. However, I wouldn't say that any kind of formal qualifications are essential for advertising copywriting.

Nigel got his first position by writing to a large number of advertising agencies asking if they had room for a trainee copywriter. He says, 'Just one did, and they took me on. I was initially teamed up with a trainee art director in a creative department of three other experienced teams who taught me a lot.'

Nigel's advice for anyone who wants to break into a career in advertising copywriting is:

> It's important to be able to think visually as well as verbally. The majority of great ads, posters and TV commercials use words and pictures in a dynamic way. Most creative directors are not just looking for a wordsmith, they are looking for someone with ideas (or concepts as they are called in the trade). You don't have to be able to draw, but you do have to be able to suggest the way that headlines and visual ideas can work together to sell a product or service.
>
> When you write, have an image in your mind of a specific person you are selling to. Think about why they need the product. Think about what they need to know. Worry about boring them. Use the language they would use. Never patronize. Keep everything crystal clear, persuasive and exciting.

Professional organizations and training providers

The Institute of Practitioners in Advertising is the trade body and professional institute for the UK's advertising, media and marketing communications industry. To become a member you need to be in the employment of a member agency. You may want to use the list of member agencies to help you when looking for work; there are also job opportunities and careers sections on the site.

The Advertising Association is a federation of trade bodies and organizations (including the IPA) representing the advertising and promotional marketing industries. It has a useful careers guide at http://www.adassoc.org.uk/Getting_into_advertising.pdf.

D&AD runs a range of educational programmes for those new to advertising and design, and continuing development workshops for those already in the industry.

Where to look for work

Trade media
If you want to look for advertising vacancies, there are a number of publications, websites and directories which focus on the right sort of jobs or list relevant agencies:

- *Campaign*
- *Marketing Week*
- *Marketing*
- *Guardian* (Monday)
- *Financial Times*
- *Advertisers Annual*
- *Writers' and Artists' Yearbook*
- Institute of Practitioners in Advertising Agency List
- Brand Republic, www.brandrepublic.com.

There are a range of different types of agency where you could find work, and large companies also have advertising departments. You are most likely to find jobs writing advertisements at a creative agency. In a direct marketing agency you could be working on direct mail or direct response radio advertising. An online or digital agency will focus on internet communication or search-engine marketing. There are also full service agencies which offer a range of services, possibly including PR and direct marketing, alongside branding and advertising.

Level of pay
The amount you can charge when freelancing in copywriting for advertisements is unlikely to be based on an amount per word. Instead, you may want to charge per day, as it can take many hours' work and plenty of revisions to come up with a short paragraph or sentence. The rate you charge will also depend on who you are working for. Large agencies and big companies with advertising departments will pay the most.

Alison Bukhari has been working in copywriting for around twenty-five years, and now runs an advertising agency, Starfish

Advertising and Marketing, www.starfish-advertising.co.uk. Alison started with a degree in business studies, specializing in marketing. She says, 'It is a massive help for a copywriter to understand business in the wider sense.' She moved into advertising from marketing, and says, 'I was the client who rewrote agency copy. I found I was usually better at it than they were. It helps to work client-side before going into an agency. It gives you a different perspective: for example, when a client is asking you to change something you can understand why.' Alison worked freelance for a short while before joining an agency. Describing her work, she says, 'Most of what I write is direct response related and as such you can measure the results of what you write. I have never been on a formal copywriting course for direct response writing. I have a natural talent for it and I learnt "on the job".'

Alison set up her advertising agency in 2000. She says:

> I had been working from home and was doing increasingly more projects for big clients – but you can't really have serious business meetings in your spare room, so it was a case of grow or go backwards. The biggest difficulties have been around staff. You can't expect them to be as committed as you are, it's not their business. But when you have a good team around you as I do now, there's a real buzz in pitching for and winning business with blue-chip clients, especially when you beat the "big boys"!'

Alongside running Starfish, Alison lectures on copywriting for response for the Institute of Direct Marketing and delivers in-company writing courses for many big companies. She has some good advice for anyone wanting to break into advertising:

> For a start, make sure you can spell and punctuate, otherwise you will be a liability to your agency and their clients. Make sure you read widely and take notice of everything that's going on in the world. Most of all, take an interest in all kinds of different people – think about what motivates them and why they behave as they do. That way you'll be able to put yourself in their shoes when you're trying to decide the best way of getting your message over to them.

With all writing you are trying to 'sell' something – whether it's a product, a service or an idea – so you have to keep a clear focus on what your objective is – no unnecessary waffling! Keep a clear picture in your mind of who you are talking to. Know what your 'proposition' is (the single sentence that sums up the benefit of what you are offering the target). Then just tell them about it in as simple and straightforward a way as possible. Easy!

Is advertising for you?

If you want to work in advertising, here are a few questions to think about:

- Do I have relevant experience and skills? This is an area where in-house experience is vital, so make sure you have some practice or training.
- Do I have an art director to work with?
- Who do I want to target with my communications service?
- Am I clear about what I can offer and my rates?
- How will I reach potential clients?

Identify areas you need to work on and plan how to do it. You will soon be on your way to making a living in advertising.

Chapter 6

Corporate communications

Big businesses require an enormous amount of written material to communicate internally to staff and externally to shareholders, customers and other stakeholders. Opportunities in this area can be well paid, largely due to the size of the corporations. Equally, you can find freelance work helping out small businesses that do not have the resources to do all their copywriting in-house.

What the job involves

If you want to write for a company, you could find yourself working on a range of different outputs. You could be responsible for an in-house newspaper or magazine, and feel that your job is much like that of a reporter. Alternatively, you could end up working exclusively online, building and maintaining a company intranet. You might need to turn dull corporate data into an attractive annual report or company brochure, or come up with lively presentations for senior staff to give.

Your personality

Corporate copywriting covers a diverse range of work, and different aspects can suit different people. If you are outgoing, you may enjoy working with a big company where the role involves lots of external and internal liaison and face-to-face communication. Introverts may prefer to pick a corporate communications role where their job is more desk based and involves writing copy. Really, in this area, the important thing is to know your strengths and focus on getting the sort of work that suits you.

More about the work

Steve Knight is Fellow of the British Association of Communicators in Business and runs Knight Train & Consult, www.knighttrain.co.uk. He trains internal communications professionals, journalists and PR staff in writing, sub-editing, design, proofreading and editorial and management skills, and has been working in corporate communications for more than thirty-five years. He says:

> Corporate communications is a wide-ranging area. You could end up looking after marketing, PR, and internal comms too; indeed, every facet of a company that needs to be communicated could come under corporate communications. In some places one person is responsible for everything, in others there are several separate teams. You could be answering media calls from the local, national or trade press one morning, arranging a managers' away day in the afternoon, and attending a corporate social responsibility event in the evening.

Whatever part of corporate communications you are in, you will need to work within a range of constraints. Businesses will have a house style which you will need to absorb, refer to and conform to. There may be tight deadlines to meet. Companies can be full of internal politics, and part of your job may be to convey a company line to employees or the outside world.

Writing style

As with many copywriting positions, you need to be flexible to be a corporate communicator. If you freelance, a writing style that works for one company will not be appropriate for another. You could be working on a detailed document for directors in the morning, and writing in a completely different style for the company intranet in the afternoon. A copywriter with thirty years' experience, Jim, says:

> It helps if you can express ideas in a punchy but clear way. Any manager can spout the current business buzz phrases. If you can turn these into something that actually means something, then you're doing something they can't do. Therefore you have to be able to grasp business or technical concepts and turn them into clear language. This is true even if you're writing for a technical audience. They get bombarded with acronym- or buzzword-laden literature all the time. If you can produce something that expresses the key ideas in a simple way, it rises above the noise. *Not* writing like a manager helps. A touch of wit never hurts.

Mark Shanahan of Leapfrog Corporate Communications comments, 'You've got to be good with words. You need to understand management-speak, and translate the message into plain English in a way that will achieve the company's aims.'

Steve Knight explains some of the difficulties of working with corporate material:

> To be a good corporate communicator, you need to be able to explain things simply. Avoid management-speak and corporate jargon. One of the biggest issues for anyone in corporate comms is that much of your material originates from highly motivated, skilled, clever senior managers who forget that their audiences may not be so informed about what they do. You need to translate *Economist*-level writing for a *Daily Mail*-level audience, otherwise

managers can appear aloof and out of touch. A good corporate communicator can make managers more real to their staff, so even if people don't like the message they trust it.

Areas of work

In-house publications
Perhaps the thing most people will first come up with when asked about corporate communications is the company newspaper or magazine. Journalism training can come in handy when you are faced with commissioning features, writing articles, subediting other people's contributions and coming up with eyecatching headlines. You may also be called upon to proofread publications, which is a skill in itself. As well as producing print media, corporate communications departments may be using e-zines which need slightly different skills. See Chapter 9 for more on journalism, and Chapter 11 for proofreading.

House magazines and contract publishing
One particular area of corporate communications is producing house magazines. There are a number of companies who specialize in creating publications, paid for by a company, to be distributed to that company's customers, clients or staff. The content of such magazines can vary enormously. Some try to provide a range of articles that you could find in any news-stand magazine, and offer the chance for people who are not company customers to subscribe. One such magazine is *Right Start*, which is provided to parents who take their children to Tumbletots as part of their subscription, and to anyone else who wants to order it.

Magazines can be commissioned as a way of getting a certain message across. The NSPCC works with Redwood Publishing to produce *Your Family*, providing positive parenting information and distributed free through Early Learning Centre stores. Other big players in this area include airlines, most of whom produce an in-flight magazine. All the major supermarkets and many other big chain stores have their own customer magazine, providing space to promote new lines and offers, among articles of interest to their readers. Some companies tailor the content to the reader group, producing several different versions of the content for older readers or those with young families, for example.

Frances writes on a regular basis for contract publishers, and says:

> Writing for contract magazine publishers varies quite a lot according to the organization behind the mag. With *Your Family* magazine, which is published on behalf of the NSPCC, there is probably less difference than with a magazine for a commercial company. The NSPCC does have a very strict editorial standpoint on certain things such as ethnic diversity in case studies, and of course it has a very child-centred point of view. But otherwise it's not that different to mainstream mags as it's not trying to sell something. I also work on a magazine for a leading store, which naturally has an agenda to promote its products,. It does tend to want to promote the feelgood factor and probably wouldn't dwell too deeply on problems. It wants the woman reading it to feel glowing, happy and upbeat – and hopefully positive about heading off to her nearest store.

Examples of contract publishers:

- Brooklands Group
- Cedar Communications
- John Brown Citrus Publishing
- PA Customer Publishing
- Redwood Group Publishing
- River Publishing
- Seven Squared Publishing.

Frances has also worked for the Prudential magazine. She describes her experience:

> One feature was about the *Titanic* and how many of the crew who

were lost had life assurance with the Pru, the first company to offer policies to the poor. This sounds very company focused but was actually a fascinating article about a whole section of society gaining access to financial security that only the middle and upper classes had known before. Other pieces were simple lifestyle pieces – for example about gardens – with no mention of the Pru at all.

As a freelancer, Frances finds working for contract publications not too dissimilar to working for other magazines, but says:

> I think the difference really shows for the editor or staff who have to liaise with the client. Clients have to see and approve all pages and there can be a battle between editorial staff and the client about how much hard sell there is. Often this is not only a copy issue but a design issue: asking for lots of pics of ugly products to be added is a sure way to irritate a designer who has lovingly crafted some gorgeous arty pages.

Frances's final piece of advice is, 'It seems that contract publishers pay better than your average parenting mag. So it's nice to have them as a solid base to your income.'

Pitching to a contract publisher has similarities with pitching to any other publication (see Chapter 9). Read the publication, and think about its ethos and its readership. However, you should also find out about how much product promotion goes into the publication, and ask the editor what they are looking for. Visit www.magforum.com/custom_publishers.htm for more information on contract publishers.

Corporate brochures and annual reports

As the company's communications expert you may be involved in producing corporate publications. If you are asked to work on an annual report, it helps if you are aware of the legal requirements in the Companies Act 2006, and other relevant legislation. The Worshipful Company of Marketors, www.marketors.org, has devised a framework to assist companies who want to ensure that their reporting complies with Accounting Standards Board requirements and at the same time assists in promoting the company to key figures in the City.

Corporate announcements and PR
When working in corporate communications you will certainly find yourself involved to a greater or lesser extent in how your company is perceived by the outside world. Public relations skills can come in handy, and some corporate communicators go on to take the Chartered Institute of Public Relations qualifications. See Chapter 8 to find out more about the skills you might need.

Training manuals and course materials
You may well find that your input is required in company training manuals. You will need to be able to write in an understandable style to a range of audiences. You may be called upon simply to edit a course manual that a subject specialist has devised, or you may need to write the manual and use your communication skills to get others involved. Margaret Burnside has been involved in training and development for twenty-four years and currently runs the Centre for Personal Development. In the course of her career she has written many training courses and advises:

There are two types of training manual – one written directly to learners to support their learning of a particular subject and the second for those who will be delivering a training course. There are some crucial differences in the types of writing required and one or two things in common. Training is about helping people to learn, so with either type of manual it is important to use a clear, technically accurate and unambiguous style. Material may also have to be translated at some point – so should be free from clichés, local dialect and UK-specific phrases, such as 'put you on the spot'. It is important to maintain a light touch, without being too casual and certainly not formal and stuffy. A suggestive tone is usually more inviting than an instructional tone; for example, 'You must complete a time log for two weeks to analyse your current use of time' might seem threatening, while, 'You might find it useful to complete a time log for a week, or even two depending on your workload ...' leaves the learner feeling that they have some choice over how they carry out this task. Use plenty of examples to illustrate key points, helping the learner to imagine how they might use this skill or technique or relate to the concepts you are explaining.

If you are writing a course for someone else to deliver, Margaret recommends:

It is usually more helpful to avoid a script and use more of a bullet point style, allowing the deliverer to use their own, more natural style. The layout can make a big difference, clearly differentiating between content and 'stage management', e.g. 'use the flipchart to illustrate this point', 'ask the groups to define "Time Management" ... 'The objective of this session is to ....'

See the example, below.

Session/time	Key Points	Resources
Session 1 Introductions 09.15–09.45	Welcome to the Time Management course Introduce self Ask delegates to introduce each other with the following information: • Name • Job Role • Hobbies Allow 5 mins discussion then ask individuals to introduce neighbour	Slides 1 and 2 Flipchart

Writing for the net

Most corporate communications departments will be running a company intranet. There may be a specialist on the team who is responsible for the site, or it may be just one more responsibility for someone. If you are taking on an intranet, there are plenty of resources to help you brush up your web writing skills. See Chapter 10 for more.

Alongside an intranet, you may need to be familiar with a whole range of technology and software as how we communicate changes. You may need to communicate with staff via their BlackBerrys, which raises issues about the length and size of messages that can be read on a small screen. You may get involved in creating a company blog, and need to know about using RSS feeds to keep up with developments on other blogs relevant to the business.

Mark Shanahan started his career as a journalist, covering finance for *Which?* magazine. Better pay enticed him to work for a building society in their PR and marketing department, which started his career in corporate communications. He moved to be Divisional Communications Manager for a bank, and was then head hunted to become Corporate Communications Manager for a large hotel chain. When the group was broken up and sold off he took redundancy, intending to freelance for a while before looking for another position. Instead, after bumping into someone who was looking for a freelancer, he ended up setting up Leapfrog Corporate Communications, www.leapfrogcomms.com. Mark explains, 'They needed someone to cover a maternity leave vacancy for five months, but wanted to contract with a company to do this. This spurred me on to set up Leapfrog, and eight years on the business is still going strong.' Leapfrog is now run by Mark and his wife. They have had employees in the past, but have found it simplest to contract with other freelancers when needed. The company mainly provides high level strategic input, often in the area of change management.

Skills

Journalism skills

Many people working in corporate communications have taken a journalism course, although this is not compulsory. Journalism skills are vital for many parts of the job, but you also need the ability to take a different perspective. Catherine Park of the British Association of Communicators in Business (CiB) says, 'With journalism, people are choosing to read something. If you are involved in internal communications you need to get everyone to read some things. Understanding your audience and what will engage them is a vital skill. You need to be attuned to your audience, yet constantly aware of what your communications are trying to achieve.'

However, there are a number of ways corporate copywriting differs from journalism. A business is paying for the communications it sends, and therefore each communication needs to be achieving something for the business. In an article, Sue Williams of the British Association of Communicators in Business says, 'The internal communicator must achieve something more than simply getting as big an audience as possible. It's that "something more" that journalism training isn't designed (in fact doesn't need) to teach.' Williams also suggests that theories of marketing can't be applied to internal comms, because of different audience dynamics. The audience has more of a duty to go through internal communications materials received at work, and hence has a different set of feelings about what they read. This becomes important when the copywriter needs to communicate health and safety matters, say, that all staff need to read. You need to be able to write copy on a range of subjects, some more interesting than others, in a way that provides compelling reading.

Strategic thinking

For almost all corporate writing, you need to be able to plan. Communication has a cost to the company, and it will be looking to achieve certain outcomes from its investment. So, whether you are writing a small flyer with a print run of a thousand or editing content for a training manual in collaboration with another department, you need to be aware of the purpose of the project. Put simply, make sure you are clear about:

- objectives
- messages
- audience
- outcomes
- measurement and evaluation.

Objectives

Corporate objectives will probably be determined at a senior level: any organization will have a number of objectives that they are working towards over a period of a year or more. You may be working at a level where you are just part of a large communications department, and are told what is required of your writing. Alternatively, you may need to come up with the plans to work towards the company objectives and get others on board.

Messages

It sounds simple, but if you are clear about the messages you need to convey your job will be much easier. Again, companies may have general messages that they want conveyed in every output, and you may have specific messages to get across with different pieces of work. If you are unclear about this, always ask the person who has requested or commissioned the work.

Assessing your target audience

As a corporate copywriter you need to be adept at assessing the audience you are writing for, using appropriate language and understanding about employee engagement. An in-house magazine or health and safety leaflet may need to be read by cleaners, company directors, secretaries, lab staff and groundspeople, all of whom will have different interests. Mark Shanahan advises, 'People who have been journalists, working on publications or websites, may have no idea of how a business works, nor of what makes people tick.' Steve Knight comments:

The range of work is huge. Thirty years ago you might just have worked on an in-house newspaper or magazine. Now intranets and internets and corporate blogs have developed. This wide range of comms vehicles has some dangers: you can end up writing several things badly instead of doing one thing well. However, the skills needed are similar for all of them. Before putting pen to paper, think about who your target audience is and what is the best way to communicate with them, and write accordingly. Do not get caught up in admiring your own writing style, or writing to impress management.

Outcomes and evaluation

It makes your job much easier if you are clear about the outcomes you need to achieve. Does the company newsletter need to inform staff about certain issues? You may need to evaluate the success of your communications, and be able to use surveys or commission focus groups to establish how informed staff and stakeholders are, and measure the effect of your communication strategy.

Technical writing

Depending on the nature of the company's business, you may need to be able to understand technical documents. Many businesses employ technical writers specifically to come up with manuals and informative text. If you have a technical background, you can use your specialist knowledge to develop a well-paid niche for your writing.

Writing by committee

When working with a business there may be a number of different departments involved in a publication. You may be needed to create a draft for circulation, and take written comments or convene a meeting to work on the copy. You may need to recruit external stakeholders to be involved in the consultation process too. You need a range of skills to do this successfully, including plenty of tact and patience. You must be able to listen and note down which suggestions are important and relevant, and keep a paper trail of how the document has developed. Some companies will have procedures to follow to help you do this: otherwise you can be caught out if someone comes back to you six months down the line to justify why some information was included or omitted. Consultation can ensure that all ideas are included, but rarely makes for a well-written document, so you can find yourself having to go back through and edit for style once all comments have been incorporated. You may then need to get final sign-off from one or more key figures.

Interviewing

If you are working in a big company or freelancing you may find yourself called upon to interview a senior figure in the company to provide a profile or document their views on a new project. You need to be able to research their background and gen up on the issue, and have an awareness of the industry or company context. Geoff Davies of WWAM Writers is a business communications writer with forty-five years' experience. He advises that the expertise that the business writer brings to a successful interview has very little to do with prior knowledge of the subject. It consists in being able to:

- ask the right questions;
- assimilate the information obtained;
- organize it in a logical structure;
- articulate it clearly;
- make it more reader-friendly;
- bring the key points to the fore; and
- ideally prompt a desired response.

It takes practice to be able to pursue ideas that have come up in the interviewee's answers while remaining aware of the topics that you need and want to cover.

Change management

Much of corporate communications can involve change management. Mark Shanahan says, 'When everything is ticking along many companies manage their communications in-house. At times of mergers and acquisitions, when businesses are changing the way they operate, large organizations look for outside help.' If you are involved in communicating change, Mark advises:

> Good writing skills are important, but you need more. You must be able to understand a business, where it is heading, how to get there and how good communications can support that. One organization I worked with had printed its core values on mouse mats and posters, and wanted me to work out why staff weren't embracing the values. We identified that the problem was that management weren't working with the core values either, and suggested that a communication campaign would not change things unless management changed the way they behaved too.

Knowledge

Corporate communications can be vital to the success of an organization, and to be a successful writer you need to be able to understand the context you are working in. It takes some skill to be able to understanding the needs of the business from the perspective of internal and external stakeholders. You need to read up in the trade media, national papers and relevant websites to understand the external agenda, and create your work with that as background. It can be vitally important to be up to date in order to make sure that your company's communications are accurate and relevant.

Understanding people

Steve Knight believes that successful corporate communicators need to have a good knowledge of how people tick. He explains:

> Understand that people don't always say what they think, especially when confronted by management. You need to like people too. Your job is often to write what staff need to know, so you need to know what interests and excites people. Don't forget about the members of staff who are just there to earn enough to pay their bills.

They won't care about the latest sales initiative unless you can show how it will affect them.

Training

There are no hard and fast rules about qualifications for corporate communications. Some people may move into communications from another area, while others have taken a degree in communications, business, marketing or a similar discipline. Mark Shanahan's advice on breaking into corporate communications is as follows: 'Increasingly you don't need a background in writing, and you can learn on the job. Some people get experience working for a comms agency, moving from job to job.' Catherine Park says, 'A communications degree is not a prerequisite, but appropriate qualifications and training are very important for progression and to help meet career challenges.' Steve Knight says, 'I'm frustrated by people who go into corporate communications without training; you can end up in a position where you don't have the knowledge to cope with the work you face. There may be no other professional communicator in your organization to ask for advice. You can't just do this successfully by reading books.'

If you do want to do some training that will help in your career, Park advises:

> Look for a professional qualification that will suit the career path that attracts you. You may want to work in communications for a while; look at the different qualifications available, then make a decision. You could opt for a diploma like that offered by Kingston University in Internal Communication Management, or choose a qualification from the Chartered Institute of Marketing or the Chartered Institute of Public Relations.

Professional organizations and training providers

The British Association of Communicators in Business

For internal communications, join the British Association of

Communicators in Business (CiB). Catherine Park of the CiB says, 'Joining CiB is good for your credibility. It shows that you are interested in professional development, best practice and keeping up to date. This is important when you are going for a job, especially if you don't have much experience.' CiB sends members a monthly magazine and separate e-zine covering topical issues. There is more information in the Knowledge Bank on the CiB website, www.cib.uk.com. In the members' area of the website there are more than fifteen how-to guides, covering skills like doing presentations, communicating change, developing an intranet and engaging employees. Park says, 'This sort of information can help you prepare for a job interview, or give you the knowledge you need when faced with an unfamiliar task. We have a members' forum too, where you can ask for advice and feedback.' CiB offers a range of regional meetings and networking events. You can get a member discount on the organization's training events, which cover topics including email newsletters, writing headlines, and writing for the web. Steve Knight advises, 'Make sure you get involved. Belonging to an organization like the CiB is especially useful if you are working on your own. Go along to events to meet other professionals and improve your own skills.'

The International Association of Business Communicators
The International Association of Business Communicators, www.iabc.com, is another professional organization which offers opportunities to network with members around the world through the website and face to face at chapter events and professional development seminars. It offers a searchable directory of members, a blog, learning resources and job listings.

Publications
Melcrum, www.melcrum.com, is a research and training business, focusing on all aspects of internal communication. It offers newsletters and job listings, and publishes *Strategic Communications Management*. Mark Shanahan subscribes and says, 'Although it is one of the more expensive publications it opens up networks and training events.'

If you work in a particular industry you need to stay on top of your trade's print media. You may also find some interesting information in *PR Week*.

Experience

Corporate comms is an area that it is possible to break into from outside. Mark Shanahan says, 'It was very noticeable that while up until the 90s people were coming into the industry from journalism, now we are seeing people from marketing, HR, or even operations becoming corporate communications specialists.' Steve Knight comments, 'I believe that if you have trained as a journalist you know how to concentrate on your audience. Journalism isn't the only way into corporate communications. Many people have started out in a different career. A PA, for example, could be asked to take on the company newsletter and end up working in communications.'

Steve Knight advises:

> If you are working in a different area, look at whether you can start contributing to the comms team in some way. If you are working in accounts, is there something in that area which could be turned into an interesting feature for the staff magazine? Contact the comms office responsible and explain how you could write about something everyone would like to know more about. If you really want to get into comms, put in the time and effort. Talk to the comms team and you may reap the reward. Remember, though, that working in comms is still hard work and don't think that the grass is always greener.

It is important to look at each position and how you can use it to develop your skills. Knight comments:

> If you genuinely want to be a good corporate communicator, look seriously at jobs, and find out who you would be working to. Is there a senior person in the team who you can learn from? If not, do you really want that job? Work with serious players and it will help

you develop the skills and gravitas you need, rather than being left on your own to flounder.

Claire Fuller of Writing Machine explains why experience is essential when working as a freelance corporate copywriter:

> All the work we do is business-to-business corporate communications and bid writing. Most of our clients are in the technology field. If we are commissioned to work on a technology case study, we will be looking for a freelancer who has written technology case studies before. There is client interaction: the freelancer would have to interview the client on the phone then write up the case study. We wouldn't want to take a chance and end up having to go back to the client if the work wasn't up to scratch.

If you don't have experience, there are posts where you can learn. Claire explains:

> In the past we have taken on junior writers and trained them up, but it takes a lot of resources, so the salary won't be great. However, it is a good way of getting hands-on experience. Lots of the copywriters we use now trained with us, moved on to other positions to get wider experience, and have returned to us as freelancers.

Claire has some advice for beginners: 'Show potential employers that you really love writing, and never send in an email or CV with a typo. Your chance of getting a job would be zero.'

Freelancing

If you want to become a freelance, corporate communications can be a good area to focus on, but make sure you get some experience. If you are new to corporate comms and want to go straight into freelancing you may not have the knowledge, background or contacts that you need to get going. Steve Knight advises, 'Try to work in two or three different jobs before looking at a freelance career.' He also has useful advice to help you succeed: 'If you are thinking about going freelance, make out a good business case for yourself. What is your Unique Selling Point? Why would people hire you instead of others?' If you are going freelance, Mark Shanahan advises, 'Define what service that you can offer that is better than anyone else's. It is a very competitive area. Before taking the plunge, make sure you develop a good network, but don't expect all those people to have the same relationship with you once you are hoping to become a supplier.' Steve Knight continues:

> Will you be able to afford to live? Work out what you need to earn over a year. Be ruthlessly honest with yourself. If you need £2,000 to pay your bills, mortgage, car, phone and computer each month, and are charging £300 a day, how many days' work must you have booked every month? Can you guarantee to get that level of work, and can you afford to ever take a holiday? Don't forget that you need to set aside a quarter of what you earn for tax.

The CiB has a freelance forum where you can pick up on work opportunities, email other members, attend freelance networking events and fairs, and be listed in a freelance directory.

Getting freelance work

There is a range of ways of getting freelance work. Mark Shanahan of Leapfrog Corporate Communications says, 'I get work direct from businesses, through design agencies and via management consultancies.' Make the most of your contacts. Steve Knight advises networking as the best way of getting work. He says, 'Go and meet people and talk to people, whether you meet them in a spa, on the golf course or in an art class. You don't need to bore them about your business; talk about what they do and be interested in people. Chance encounters can lead to amazing opportunities.'

Once you have made a contact, nurture it. Steve Knight explains: 'Don't send out random emails. If you do need to get in touch with someone, send an email and follow up with a phone call. I always reply to every email and phone call I get, which helps people trust me and know I do what I say I'm going to do.'

And, as with all freelancing, be persistent. It can take twenty emails, and ten phone calls before you get some work. Stick at it, build up your reputation for quality work delivered on time, and you will succeed.

Jim

Jim has been writing for nearly thirty years, and combines a mix of commercial copywriting with photography and book writing. He says, 'After a degree in fine art photography I worked briefly as a photographic assistant to a well-known advertising photographer before landing a job on a camera mag. There I reviewed cameras, etc., and got into journalism that way.' After that he worked on photography and IT mags as a writer, including on part-works, then moved into defence and other corporate areas. Jim says:

> I've nearly always been freelance and have only been salaried a couple of times in my career. These days I mainly work for large corporates, editing magazines and creating marketing materials. My corporate work goes in phases, with very busy periods, then nothing for weeks as the publications tend to be quarterly. I'm either working like crazy, or focusing mainly on creative photography and writing a novel. I do some PR work which tends to have short deadlines and quick turnarounds.

Jim works from France, and goes back to the UK to meet clients a few times a year but does most of his networking via email, with some phone conferencing.

Jim says:

> I've lucked into a lot of this work. Tackle those business sectors you know well first, so that you can talk the talk and demonstrate that you have a grasp of concepts, issues – the things that are keeping people awake at night in either fear or excitement. Other than that, I think it's probably the usual thing of getting yourself out there and getting noticed. Oh, and it's important that your website, pitch

letters, even your CV, demonstrate exactly the kind of pithy, witty, high-impact writing that people need from you.

Is corporate communications for you?

If you think you want to work in corporate communications, here are a few questions to think about:

- Do I have relevant experience and skills, or how can I get some practice or training?
- Who do I want to target with my communications service?
- Am I clear about what I can offer and my rates?
- How will I reach potential clients?

Make a plan to help work through the issues raised by these questions and you will soon be ready to start making a living in corporate communications.

Chapter 7

Marketing

Are you interested in working out what people want, and being paid by a company to create persuasive copy about how their goods and services can meet those wants? If so, you might enjoy working in marketing. Marketers use a wide range of methods to reach people, with the aim of helping a business to grow.

Marketing differs from public relations or advertising in that much of it aims to reach consumers directly, without going via print or broadcast media. However, most marketing campaigns will be running alongside advertising and public relations programmes, all hoping to achieve overlapping and complementary objectives for the business.

What the job involves

Working for an agency
You will benefit from spending some time working for a marketing agency to get a good idea of the possibilities in marketing. Scott Knox, managing director of the Marketing Communications Consultants Association (MCCA) says, 'A copywriter role in a direct marketing agency is an area where you need creative writing skills. If you want to move into marcomms, you need to prove

that you have the ability to think creatively and commercially.'

You could become a specialist copywriter in a larger agency. Account managers would commission you to come up with exciting copy ideas for a client's project. This would allow you to spend more time writing, but you would have less control over the project. You may still need to be able to present your ideas, and will need good teamwork skills. As in advertising, a marketing copywriter may spend a lot of time working in a team with an art director. Knox continues:

Working as a copywriter in marcomms, you tend to need to pair off with a partner who is an art director. In big, London-based agencies it is rare to see people move in from another sector, and people rarely get jobs without being in a creative partnership. If you need to find a partner, I'd suggest spending time at your local art college. Talk to people learning graphic or digital design. If you already have some writing experience, offer your writing skills to a student and work on projects together. The harsh reality is that you will spend a lot of time finding a partner and building a portfolio before you have even secured a job.

See Chapter 5 for more about getting experience and finding an art director to partner you.

A marketing agency can be a fast-paced place to work, with demanding deadlines. You may find yourself working as an account handler, where you need to be able to multitask. This is not a job for someone who just wants to sit and write. You will be liaising with a range of departments, listening to the client, keeping them up to date and using your presentation skills to sell your ideas to them. You may need to brainstorm for a new campaign, write a creative brief, commission or sign off artwork. Scott Knox comments:

Some big London agencies are very traditional and you never find people crossing over from the account handling side to the creative side. However, smaller agencies may be more flexible. There are more people moving round the sector doing different roles. Look at smaller agencies outside London and you may find a business that is willing to take on an account handler with experience outside marketing, and you may find your role involves more writing and creating marketing materials.

Charities and the public sector

Many charities will also have a marketing department. You may be doing the same sort of tasks as in an agency, but charities usually have a different, possibly more relaxed, culture than the private sector. Charities and public sector organizations may also commission a marketing agency to do some or all of their promotional work.

Freelancing

There are many opportunities for freelance marketing. You could use contacts from previous marketing positions and freelance for marketing agencies, filling in where they need extra cover. You may set yourself up offering marketing services and advice to small businesses that do not have a marketing department of their own. Either way you will need to have a sound knowledge of marketing, be able to assess what is needed rapidly, and then carry it out. You may need to be able to plan marketing campaigns or simply implement a campaign someone else has planned. As a freelance marketer you need to have a range of skills. Claire Fuller of Writing Machine says:

A good marketing copywriter will be well aware of the fundamentals. They will understand about writing for a target audience, and be able to write to a brief. They should be able to write to the required word count too, and always meet deadlines. In a commercial world you need to be able to edit your work. When commissioning, we will always go to the freelancer who is easiest to work with, not the one who complains when a client changes the time for an interview five minutes before it is due. Where the client is paying, you need to be able to take on board their changes without a problem.

Sectors

Marketing jobs tend to be focused on a particular sector. If working for a marketing agency, you could find yourself mainly working on any one of the following:

- Agriculture
- Business
- Construction
- Consumer durables
- Financial services
- FMCG – fast-moving consumer goods
- Food and drink
- Leisure
- Media and interactive
- Medical
- Motors
- Retail
- Telecoms
- Travel.

Whether you are working in the private or public sector, on marketing goods or services, you will need plenty of creativity and good ideas to succeed in marketing. What is more, you will need to be happy to attend events, meet with clients and stand up and pitch or make a presentation. Good writing skills can make an enormous difference to marketing materials, but do remember that most marketing jobs involve a lot more than writing.

Your personality

Marketing has a range of roles to suit different personalities. An account handler must be versatile, good at organizing, negotiating and communicating with a range of people. A good marketing copywriter needs to be imaginative and creative. You need the skills to be able to think yourself into someone else's mind. However, when working for clients it is important to be able to take their feedback and criticism, so you need to develop a thick skin and be able to smile at the people who are paying your fees.

You also need an eye for accuracy and detail, and the ability to build good working relationships with suppliers. Claire Fuller of Writing Machine says, 'There are also personal characteristics which make a good freelancer. Be accommodating, and don't be too precious about the creative process.'

Louisa Bird
Louisa Bird enjoyed languages and literature at school, and then studied German at university before becoming a freelance technical translator. She enjoyed being self-employed, and developed an interest in marketing, initially when she was looking for ideas for promoting her own services. Louisa says:

> I read *Guerrilla Marketing*, by Jay Conrad Levinson, which is aimed at small businesses. I then went on to qualify in Guerilla Marketing with one of his trainers in the UK. I've also undertaken some training with CIM – the Certificate in Marketing and the E-Marketing Award – but found it more aimed at large corporates rather than the micro businesses and small businesses making up my target market.

By this point, Louisa had become interested in sharing her knowledge of marketing. She explains, 'I thought I might offer marketing coaching and consulting, but having taken some time to reflect realized that wouldn't suit my personality. As an introvert I find talking to people draining rather than invigorating, so I looked for a different way to offer marketing services.' Louisa went on to set up a website offering expert advice on marketing, the Women's Marketing Forum.

Writing style

You will need to be versatile when writing for marketing. It helps if you are able to write in a range of styles and are good at editing your own prose. In marketing you need to know which words and phrases will get the reader to take action, whether you want them to make a call, visit a website or buy something in a store. You could find yourself writing for a small space in a leaflet or promotional postcard, so need to be expert at cutting text to fit without losing the message. Louisa Bird has some tips for writing good marketing copy. She says:

> First, your copy needs to speak to your audience, so work out who you want to reach and try to get inside their head. Try to figure out what they want to hear. Think about the ideal customer, the most profitable one, and work out what they want to know about, then write about the benefits that will appeal to them. Make sure that your copy is crisp. I tend to write sentences that are too long, so I go back and chop them into two or three parts. This is vital if you are writing web copy. The eye struggles to read long lines of the written word on screen.

You could find yourself writing for any one of a number of different outputs including:

- direct mail
- coupon flyers
- insert leaflets
- sales letters
- newsletters
- postcards
- door hangers.

More and more you will find marketers involved in creating online marketing, such as emails, internet banner ads and pay-per-click ads.

Direct marketing

Direct marketing involves sending messages direct to consumers. You need the skills to be able to persuade someone who has just had a flyer fall out of a magazine or drop through their letterbox, or picked up a leaflet at random, that what is being offered is something that they want. There are specialist direct mail and direct marketing agencies who will devise and implement marketing for clients. Direct mail relies heavily on the Royal Mail as the sole 'media owner' in this sector. Direct marketing can also cover sales promotion, merchandizing, point of sale and field marketing.

The target audience for your marketing materials will not have asked to receive what you are writing so you need to work hard to make them want to read it. You must be able to write really compelling copy, and make the key message stand out. Neil Francis is a Creative Partner at direct marketing agency Stephens Francis Whitson. His agency creates copy and visuals for online and offline marketing, including mailpacks, press, banners, websites, brochures, letters and advertising. When asked what makes a copy-writer stand out Francis responds:

> The people who stand out to me make me love reading what they have written, and can write something that hooks me, and persuades me to take action. Another trait I like is the ability to take yourself out of your writing. For some people, you can always tell when they are the copywriter behind a piece, but good copy is not about you and your writing style. You need to be able to write in different ways for different jobs. On a more basic note, I like copy-writers who are punctual and can spell. You also need people who can think about things differently, and find an insight or different way to hook a reader's attention.

Benefits and features

To write good marketing copy you need to be clear about benefits and features. Many pieces of promotional literature fail because they concentrate on the features. When asked what is good about a product, the company that has developed it may well focus on its characteristics, but the person buying it needs to know, 'What will it do for me?' It is important to know and understand the needs of the target audience for the product or service you are marketing so you can understand the benefits which might appeal to them. You may need to commission surveys or focus groups, if the company budget is large enough, to help you better understand consumers' motivation around the product you are working on.

Creating a call to action

In marketing, you need to write copy with a specific purpose. In advertising you are sometimes encouraging readers or viewers to buy, and sometimes simply raising their awareness of a new brand or product, whereas marketing is almost always focused on a purchase.

The copy that you write has to create a desire for the product or service, and include a strong and focused 'call to action'. Marketing campaigns need to be developed with clear objectives, and ways of tracking responses: think about the codes you see on catalogues and leaflets.

Telemarketing

In telemarketing the sales team call potential customers over the phone to sell them a product or service. Calls may be cold, or to people who have already indicated an interest in the business offer. You may wonder where writing comes into telemarketing: each telephone conversation is carefully scripted and script writing is a specialist skill. You need to know all about the product, and also be able to understand the people who will be receiving the call. You need to be able to write as people will speak, using words and phrases that will motivate people to buy. There needs to be some scope for the person making the call to inject their own style, and make the call sound natural: you may yourself have received calls where it is all too obvious that the script in simply being read.

Angela Ireland runs her own telemarketing business, www.angelaireland.co.uk, which means that she uses a wide range of marketing skills. She writes case studies, press releases and promotional leaflets among other marketing materials. Angela says:

> To succeed in marketing, you need good people skills, an excellent telephone manner, and to be organized and methodical. You will need to develop a very good understanding of the breadth of exper-tise that is needed as there are many strands to marketing. You should also have the ability to adapt to fit in with a potential customer's brief. Additionally, to make your business succeed, you

146

need to be able to make local connections and play an active part in networking groups.

Angela has some suggestions to help you if you are writing marketing materials. She says, 'Take a step back and think what you would feel if it landed on your doormat or in your inbox; is it self-explanatory, is there jargon? Does it sound contrived or does it flow?'

Skills

Like many media jobs, anyone working in marketing needs good workload management skills. You must be able to organize, plan and prioritize. As you will be working for clients, whether you are working in a large agency or running your own business single-handed you will need to be able to complete projects efficiently in a short time, and prove to clients that you are providing cost-effective services which get results.

Research skills
Marketing plans are based on market research. To work in marketing you need to be able to find information from a range of sources, and work out what it means for your client's offering. You may need to be able to commission research as well, to find out about consumer behaviour and consumer views on the product or service you are planning for. Additionally, you will need to be able to research and understand the media landscape, part of the context in which your marketing campaign will take place. See Chapter 5 for a brief overview of UK media.

Relationship building
A large part of any marketing position is about building relationships. Whether you are working for yourself or as part of an agency you will have to develop and maintain relationships with clients. To keep people coming back you will need to execute your work in a way that exceeds their expectations.

As well as with clients, you will develop relationships with complementary businesses. You will need reliable designers and printers, and links with agencies that can create or book advertising, or come up with a public relations campaign to support your marketing. Building and maintaining business relationships is an invaluable skill to develop. You may also need good negotiation skills to help you encourage clients to take up the plan you suggest, and in order to get the best deals when procuring marketing materials.

Planning

In order to plan a successful marketing campaign, you need to have clear objectives, and understand the target audience (see 'Target audiences' in Chapter 5 and 'Strategic thinking' in Chapter 6). Once you have some basic facts you will need to come up with a plan of promotional activities. You may need to add in PR and advertising to your marketing plan, selecting appropriate media to work with. You will need to be able to make your plan meet a budget and demonstrate that you are getting the client good value for money.

Presentation skills

Once you have gathered information, you may need to present a proposal to a client. You will need to be able to create illustrative graphs and slides, and stand up and sell your proposal to decision-makers.

Implementing and evaluating a marketing plan

If you are working for a large agency you may have a team to carry out marketing activities, or commission others to do them on your behalf. In a smaller business, or if you work freelance, you need the skills to be able to carry out your marketing plans. As part of your plan you should have built in a way to gather information on success. Finally, you will need to be able to evaluate your results and report back to the client on what the marketing has achieved.

Knowledge

Four Ps and the marketing mix
If you are looking to brush up on marketing theory, think about the four Ps. For around five decades these have been used to form a basis of marketing plans. The four Ps are:

- *Product* Think about how the product relates to the user's desires. Consider the brand name, whether the product does what it claims, and if it is appealing in itself and in its packaging. You may also want to look at quality and safety issues.
- *Price* Consider the cost to the purchaser. There are different pricing strategies that you should understand such as:
   ○ Skimming – where a product is initially priced high to skim off those who will pay more to be the first to own a product.
   ○ Penetration – where a product is priced low to increase the size of the market or develop a market share.
  You will also need to think about discount strategies, volume discounts and wholesale pricing.
- *Promotion* Under this heading look at the whole marcomms mix, including advertising, sales promotions and point of sale, word of mouth and public relations.
- *Placement* In this section, you need to assess how the product gets to the purchaser. This could cover retailing online or in store.

For each element, you need to assess how it relates to your target market, and also understand the external constraints. There are limits to the four Ps, especially as marketing has changed enormously over the last fifty years, and you may find yourself marketing far more services and fewer tangible products than when the theory was created. Always look at the whole picture and see whether there are elements that have not been included by the four Ps.

Market research
Market research is essential to help you work out what consumers

want. It can be expensive: the more people whose views you want to find the higher the cost, but also the more reliable the findings. Psychology, sociology, and qualitative and quantitative research skills all come into play in market research, and it is valuable to have an understanding of these areas.

Marketing strategy

How is your company or the company you are working for standing up compared to competitors? What makes your products or services different? How can marketing make consumers choose your product over others? As you move up in your marketing career you need to have a good understanding of marketing strategy.

Louisa Bird of the Women's Marketing Forum has four essential tips for would-be marketers:

- *Know what marketing is* Marketing is not about pushing a brand name out there to anyone who will listen, it is about building relationships. Invest time, energy and imagination into starting and developing closer ties with potential, current and past customers.
- *Know what your message is, from the potential customer's point of view* Before you can start building any kind of relationship with potential customers, you need to be clear about what makes them tick, what they want (not necessarily the same as what they need), what challenges and problems they face, and, specifically, what benefits and solutions your product or service offers them.
- *Know who you want to communicate with* To ensure maximum marketing success, you need to know who precisely is going to be most useful (and profitable) for you to be communicating with in your marketing. Take some time to identify who the client's perfect customers are, then you can identify where you are likely to be able to find them (for example, where they hang out online, what they read, what other companies they do business with).
- *Know what the ultimate aim of marketing is* All your marketing

should be aimed at just one thing: making a profit. So make sure that you optimize your marketing efforts by using methods that:

- o build relationships with customers, because the most effective way of creating a profitable business is to develop a customer base of repeat buyers;
- o are most likely to provide the highest return on investment.

Regulation of marketing

There is a whole raft of regulations for marketing of specific industries and products, so it pays to gen up on the sector you want to work in. In particular, check out:

- The Data Protection Act 1998 which governs the use of personal information by businesses and other organizations. You need to ensure that data is kept securely and for no longer than it is needed. In the arena of marketing, individuals need to be told what their data will be used for and whether marketing lists will be shared with other organizations. They will probably have ticked boxes to allow this or to opt out from receiving marketing materials. Find out more about the principles of data protection on the Information Commissioner's Office (ICO) website, www.ico.gov.uk.
- The Privacy and Electronic Communications (EC Directive) Regulations 2003 govern electronic marketing, by email or by telephone. These regulations affect any business that uses cookies on a website or that operates telephone or other directories. Consumers need to be able to access contact details if you are sending out marketing materials or making marketing calls.

Email marketing regulation

Email marketing can only be sent to people who have opted in to receive it. Existing customers are considered to have opted in, known as the 'soft opt-in'. People who get your email marketing messages must be able to opt out at the point where you collect their details and in every message you send them. It is slightly different if you are sending marketing emails to organizations: the organization does not have to have consented to receive the email, but you must still provide an opt-out option.

Telephone and fax marketing regulation
The Telephone Preference Service allows consumers to opt out of getting telemarketing calls. You need people's opt-in to receive automated calls, pre-recorded phone messages and promotional faxes. The Fax Preference Service also provides an opt-out service. See www.tpsonline.org.uk and www.fpsonline.org.uk.

You can look up legislation on the Office of Public Sector Information website, www.opsi.gov.uk, or take one of the marketing courses mentioned later in this chapter.

Financial services and health marketing regulations
Some areas require more regulation than others. Financial services and health are just two areas with their own specific requirements. In healthcare, the Medicines and Healthcare products Regulatory Agency, www.mhra.gov.uk, is there to ensure that 'Advertising or marketing claims for medicines and "medical devices" are justified and targeted at appropriate audiences.' Marketing agencies responsible for healthcare products liaise closely with the MHRA to ensure marketing materials and advertisements are approved before use. In the financial arena, the Financial Services Authority, www.fsa.gov.uk, has a 'Treating Customers Fairly' initiative. The FSA says, 'We want firms to consider, when preparing promotions:

- whether the material is clear, fair and not misleading;
- whether it provides a balanced picture of the product or service;
- whether the marketing matches what the product or service delivers; and
- whether the promotions will be easily understood by their customers.'

The Authority also asks companies promoting financial services to look at whether the marketing for a particular product or service is monitored by senior management. The FSA itself monitors advertisements and promotional materials to make sure they do not break its rules.

Neil Francis says:

> If you're a budding copywriter, you need to be passionate about language and writing. To work in direct marketing you need to be interested in different things. In your role you may be writing about home insurance in the morning, and moving on to create copy about a supermarket or food product in the afternoon. You need an interest in research and discovery, and an essential inquisitiveness. You also have to love ideas. Part of the fun of this industry is the creative expression of ideas in words, pictures and a combination of both. You also need the ability to write good English and hold an argument in anything from a series of bullet points to a long company brochure. There are many different tasks involved. You could be writing for a website, in which case you need to be short and succinct. You could then move on to create a mail pack with a letter in a totally different tone of voice. We look for copywriters who show the ability to change from style to style. You also need a chameleon-like ability to slip into other people's heads.

As in advertising, in direct marketing you will often work in a team together with an art director. Neil Francis says, 'Sometimes I'll be looking to hire a team, while on other occasions I will just need a copywriter.' He advises:

> Team up with an art director. You may end up seeing more of your creative partner than you do of your husband or wife. Sign up with a number of agencies. If I'm looking for a copywriter, I may use a recruitment consultant. We look at the graduates coming out of relevant college courses, and those who are on the summer schools we arrange with the IPA.

Professional organizations and training providers

There are several organizations within the marketing arena.

The Chartered Institute of Marketing offers an accreditation scheme, allowing you to work towards a Professional Certificate in Marketing, Professional Diploma in Marketing, and Professional Postgraduate Diploma in Marketing, and a continuing professional development scheme to enable you to become a chartered marketer. Choose the Professional Diploma if you already have a degree in any subject. Courses are offered across the UK. You can choose from part-time or distance learning, as well as intensive or residential courses. The CIM also offers an innovative arrangement of 'blended learning', where part of your studies are done online, and part in class. If you can get a job in marketing while you are studying you may find that your employer will sponsor you to do the course. The CIM offers a marketing information line, and a marketing library for members. Members get *Marketer* monthly magazine and a weekly news email, plus access to local branch events for networking. The CIM also runs training courses, and offers members a free legal helpline and discounted professional indemnity insurance. It also publishes a list of chartered members.

The Marketing Society runs events with marketing specialists from leading UK businesses, produces magazines *Market Leader* and *Think* and includes a subscription to *Marketing* as part of your membership. See www.marketing-society.org.uk.

The Marketing Communications Consultants Association, MCCA, is made up of marcomms agencies, and mainly offers services to help agencies develop. It has useful advice for graduate jobseekers on its website and a list of vacancies from member agencies, and its directory of members may help you find companies to approach when you want to get experience or find work. It also looks for graduates for positions at member agencies. It offers brand owners an agency-finding service, and offers member agencies services such as workshops on procurement. It offers 'pitch protection', a service where pitches can be registered so there are no disputes at a later stage about where promotional ideas originated. See www.mcca.org.uk to find out more.

The Direct Marketing Association, www.dma.org.uk, campaigns and promotes best practice in direct marketing. It offers members networking opportunities, seminars and sector-specific forums, and sends out regular bulletins. Members also get free personalized legal and best-practice advice on direct marketing issues, plus a listing in the DMA directory. The DMA also manages the Telephone, Fax and Mailing Preference Services.

The Institute of Sales Promotion offers personal and corporate membership. Personal members get to use the letters MISP after their name, and have access to information on sales promotion policy development, best-practice guides and draft proposals for legislation, as well as the ISP reference library. The ISP holds members' events too. Students and those who are new to direct marketing can apply for associate membership. Both members and non-members can, for a fee, use the ISP's legal advice services on promotional copy clearance and industry guidelines. Find out more about the ISP at www.isp.org.uk.

Essential reading

There are plenty of magazines and websites to keep you up to date on the latest developments in marketing. The fast changing digital arena makes it essential to stay on top of the latest ways to reach people. Read Chapter 5 on advertising too, as some of the magazines mentioned there also include marketing news and jobs.

Other magazines:

- from Brand Republic (www.brandrepublic.com)
- *Marketing*
- *Marketing Today*
- *Marketing Week*
- *Revolution* (new media magazine for marketers).

Marcom Professional is a social professional network – similar to social networks like Facebook, but for anyone in the communications field. It allows you to network, collaborate with colleagues and blog, and of course hear other views on the latest in marcomms: www.marcomprofessional.com.

Experience

Getting work

As with many of the sectors covered in this book, it can seem daunting when you are looking for a job in marketing or considering going freelance. Neil Francis says:

> It is not as easy as it should be to get into the industry. In the last fifteen or twenty years there has been a shift away from hiring people out of university. People have felt that they had to go to art college, even if they wanted to get into copywriting, as the industry has been very visually led. This has not helped to attract writing talent. I'll welcome the reintroduction of a copy test to enable us to screen anyone for creative writing and thinking talents.

Starting from scratch

There is no single way into the marketing industry. A communications degree is not necessary, and qualifications like the Chartered Institute of Marketing's certificates and diplomas can be studied while you work. Look at the organizations and publications listed above to find job ads, and you'll see the wide range of jobs on offer, names of agencies, and qualifications required. Read the publications regularly and start looking at textbooks on marketing too. Neil Francis advises, 'You'll need a portfolio of work. Individual agencies vary enormously. Some won't consider entrants from outside the industry, but a lot do offer placements which can help you get started.'

If you are already working in a large company with a marketing department, look out for vacancies at the appropriate level as this may be a good way to start. Your company knowledge and interest in marketing could make up for a lack of experience.

Going freelance in marketing

If you have some experience and have worked in marketing or a similar discipline for a number of years, you may be thinking about going freelance. Neil Francis says:

> I have about fifteen freelance copywriters and a similar number of art directors who I call in on a regular basis. A lot are people I have met through work, so I would say the best way to get started is to spend a number of years in an employed position at an advertising agency. This gives you the best chance to make contacts, build your portfolio, and hopefully win a couple of awards.

Francis continues:

> Anyone who thinks that they can start as a freelancer without industry experience is making things harder for themselves. As a freelancer you get pulled into an agency on short-term projects, and don't necessarily get to see things through to the end. If you are new and looking to build up your portfolio, you won't always get the finished item to put in your book. There may be some people who have successfully started as freelancers, but far more will have gained agency experience first.

There are lots of positive points for freelancing, and marketing can be a lucrative area to work in. Many small businesses need help with their promotional planning and materials, and are happy to call in someone with specialist knowledge. You need to have a good portfolio of work, again. If you want to get into marketing, Louisa Bird advises, 'The proof of the pudding is in the eating. While qualifications are important, what really counts is being able to demonstrate examples of great marketing copy, even if you have to do a little work free of charge to build up a portfolio.'

Aim to develop your portfolio so you can demonstrate something relevant for the different industries that you are targeting, and also for different sizes of business. Work done for blue-chip companies with well-known brand names will impress, but if your bread-and-butter work comes from smaller businesses, have examples of what you have done in that area on your website too.

Planning freelance work

Look at earlier chapters for advice on planning your work and setting rates. Do some market research and check the rates of other freelancers in your area. You may be able to charge more if you offer a specialist service or have scarce industry knowledge. Sound clients out about your rates: 'Would an hourly rate of £50 be acceptable?' You won't necessarily get it right first time and some clients will be able to pay more than others. Work out how much you need to earn to pay the bills, not forgetting to allow for the costs of running your business, tax and National Insurance. Calculate how many paid hours you would have to work to earn that much at your proposed hourly rate. Don't forget that for every few hours that you work, you may need to spend an hour or so on admin, and factor that into your calculations. Guesstimate how much paid work you will actually be able to generate. As Neil Francis says, 'Freelance copywriting can be patchy work. When agencies are busy they will call you in but when budgets get cut you won't be wanted.'

If you are offering freelance marketing services, you may well need to commission other people to do some work for you. When working out costs for a job, factor in a percentage on top of the fee that you are charged by your graphic designer or printer, for example, to cover your time setting up, negotiating and troubleshooting during the procurement of marketing materials.

Freelancing for an agency can give you a decent rate of pay. If Neil Francis is looking for a freelance copywriter, he says:

> I need someone with talent who can come in and start work straight away, without needing to be told every step. You need to be familiar with the system, which is quite similar from one agency to another, and be able to work unsupervised. You must also be able to get up to speed rapidly on the thinking behind a brand, and be able to write for that brand very quickly.

Is marketing for you?

If you think you want to develop a marketing career, ask yourself:

- Do I have relevant experience and skills, or how can I get some marketing practice or training?
- Who do I want to target with my marketing service?
- Am I clear about what I can offer and my rates?
- How will I reach potential clients or agencies?

Make a plan to help work through the issues raised by these questions and you will soon be ready to start making a living in marketing.

Chapter 8

Public relations

Public relations, or PR, is about promoting news, a product or a service on behalf of a client. A public relations professional will be able to look at potential news stories and work out how to make them newsworthy enough to generate interest from journalists. Then, they contact the relevant media and persuade them to cover the story.

Where do copywriters come in?

There are a handful of marcomms roles that will let you use your creativity and writing skills and, according to Scott Knox of the MCCA, account handling in PR is one of them. He says:

> The job involves writing interesting copy that can be placed easily. If you want to work for a top ten PR agency, you can find that you still need a good degree from one of the top universities. However, there are lots of other forward-thinking agencies who might be interested in someone who has a good knowledge of blogging and even something like Second Life. They are aware of the growing role of user-generated content, and if you can show understanding of how this can be used successfully in PR, and write without sounding over-corporate, you have a chance.

There are also plenty of opportunities for freelance PR work for small and medium businesses that can't afford or don't want to have an in-house PR team, and big businesses who need extra PR help for events and launches.

To work in PR, you need to know how to write a press release, which spells out key details of the news story, usually over one to two sides of A4, in a format that is recognized by journalists. There is also a need for copy for materials to back up a PR campaign. Have a look at a real advertisement below from a PR company in search of a writer to see more about the work and skills required:

Job title: News and feature writer/PR executive
Salary: Negotiable according to experience
We want to recruit a great writer, preferably with a couple of years' experience. The range of work is extensive, from press releases to major interviews and articles and speeches. We also produce several company magazines and so there is also proofreading and magazine management thrown into the pot. You will be dealing with people from across the world on a daily basis and will have the opportunity for international travel. We are looking for an organized, computer-literate and energetic person; someone with quick, considered responses, good command of English, and a desire to excel. Being presentable and good with people is also an important part of getting the best from interviewees. An ability to get your head around technical issues will be a bonus.

Personality

If you want to work in PR you need to be creative and full of ideas. You have to be happy on the telephone and making contact with new people. You need to be able to cope with a certain amount of repetitive work: doing a ring round of key media people will involve saying the same thing over and over again, and often getting knocked back.

Writing style

In PR, you need to be able to write to a formula. You need to be able to sum up a story in a way to get a journalist's attention in a paragraph or less. You will be able to spot and edit out flowery descriptions and sales-y copy.

What other skills might you need?

If you want to use your writing skills in the PR arena, you need to recognize that you will get more work if you also have other talents. Anyone wanting to work with PR companies should be prepared to pick up the phone and sell a story. Publicity stunts and events can also form part of the work of a PR company, and you may want to think about whether you are prepared to offer help with this sort of promotional activity.

Fiona

Fiona works as a freelance writer, and offers a range of services to help businesses with PR. She says:

> I was mainly writing features when someone asked if I knew how a press release should look. I'd worked in a press office before, so it was easy to turn this small company's news story into a press release. I gave them some advice on how to send it out too. This company mentioned on an online business forum how I had helped, and after that, other businesses got in touch. I found that there was a real demand for help in turning a company's news into a release that would get coverage in their local paper.
>
> I had a website with examples of my features on it anyway, so I added some more pages with examples of the PR work I had done. As well as writing the releases, some companies wanted help selling in their story, and I quickly had to work out rates for that too. I mentioned what I offered on more business forums, and did some networking in real life, and found that I was spending more time on PR than other sorts of writing. The nice thing for me is that people approach me to help with PR, whereas with feature writing I could spend many hours pitching a story. PR has turned out to be a better source of a steady income for me.

Knowledge

If you want to break into writing for public relations, here is a quick guide to some of the essential knowledge.

Writing a press release

A press release is a newsworthy story, which is sent to newspapers, radio, television or magazines. Press releases follow a standard format. This makes it easy for a journalist to see what the story is about at a glance.

Subject

The most important part of writing the release is coming up with the newsworthy story. If you are working for a client, they may have ideas about what they want you to write. You can simply take their ideas and turn them into a press release. However, if you want the client to use you again because the release you wrote generated great publicity, look critically at the 'news' they suggest basing the release on.

Find out what publications or programmes they want the release to go to. Read the target publications, watch or listen to the programmes. Are they covering the sort of story your client is proposing? If not, you need to think of other angles and discuss different stories, or even different target audiences. Find more on target audiences later in this chapter.

It may be nice to think that a national broadsheet would be interested in a story about a small business, but would it be better directed at the local paper? This is where 'client-handling' skills come into play. Everything about the business may seem interesting to the business owner, but editors and journalists receive hundreds of press releases each day, and as a PR professional it is your job to ensure that the release is newsworthy, appropriate to the publication, and stands out from the hundreds of others that arrive on a journalist's desk on a daily basis.

Knowing news

Are you clear about what makes news? This is a vital skill to develop if you want to write press releases or work in PR. Find a pile of magazines and newspapers. Read through the publications, looking at the news pages. You might also want to check out pages highlighting new products or services, the women's section or business pages depending on whether you are focusing your writing services on a specialist area. Look at the stories and ask yourself:

- What is the main point of the story?
- Who does the story interest?
- What makes the story 'newsworthy' and worth covering?

Jot down your answers and see if you come up with any trends. Are the publications covering shocking events, innovative products, personal scandal? What makes a good serious business story? Think about this when you are reading or watching a programme as it will help you improve the services you can offer clients if you have a good nose for news.

Hooks and headlines

All releases need a 'hook' or 'angle', something that will appeal to editors and give your story a good chance of gaining coverage. Journalists are always on the look-out for stories that will interest the readers of their paper or magazine.

The first sentence of the press release needs to instantly capture the journalist's attention and sum up the story. Use the first paragraph to answer all the important questions, like who, what, where, when, why and how. Get vital information in first, so if the journalist stops reading after the first paragraph, he or she has a good idea of the story.

Write in the style of the magazine you are targeting. Editors may just take your words and put them straight on the page. It can help if you focus on a problem you are solving for readers.

Andy Turner runs Six Sigma PR, www.sixsigma-pr.co.uk. Here he shares his tips for good copywriting. 'Short words instead of long ones. Short sentences too. Make sure you properly understand your audience and write in an appropriate tone and style. Think carefully about why a busy reader should read your words instead of the thousands of others clamouring for attention; address this early on in whatever you are producing.'

Once you have the essentials of the story, make sure you have a brief but attention-grabbing headline. If you are emailing the press release this may be the first, or only, part of the release that a journalist reads. It's up to you to decide just how much information needs to be in the headline to interest them enough to read on.

Then back up your claims with facts and statistics in the following paragraphs. In general, when writing press releases it is best to use facts and cut back on adjectives. Always use the present tense or the release can sound like old news, and write in the third person ('he' or 'she', instead of 'I'). Include short quotes, in italics, highlighting new information that is not mentioned elsewhere in the press release.

Writing for print or email?

Most press releases are sent by email now. Bear this in mind when working out paragraph length and spacing. One way to check a release is to paste it into an email and send a copy to yourself. Can you see the key points of your story in the reading pane of your email program? If not, you may need to adjust the opening of the press release to get to the main story right away.

Alternatively, the release you are writing may be going into a media pack or be sent by post with samples. In this case it is important that all the key information, and probably a small clear image fits into the first page. If you have more than one page, number the pages, and put 'Page 1 of 2' or 'More, over' at the bottom of the first page so journalists know to read on. Finish the press release with ### ENDS ###.

In general, you should keep press releases to one or two sides of A4, double-spaced to give the editor room to scribble. Double spacing is less critical, however, if you are emailing a release. Use a clear modern font like Ariel, at least 10pt in size. Make paragraphs short for easy reading and align the text to the left.

Notes at the end

Whether you are writing a press release for print or email, it should always include a section at the end titled 'Notes to editors'. This should incorporate the PR contact's phone number, the company address, name, fax number, email and website. Include the hours that the contact is available at the listed phone number and add an after-hours phone number, if you can. You should also state whether there are photographs available to back up the story.

You may want to have a short section of background information on the company, when it was launched, its achievements and any awards in the 'Notes to editors'. It can be clearest to have these notes as a series of numbered points. An example of a press release is opposite.

Multiple media

If you are targeting different media sectors with the same story, write multiple releases rather than issuing one 'catch-all' release. Make sure you scan different publications to get an idea of the style they prefer. If you are doing more than just writing the release this will also help when you need to find a contact to target with the release.

Target audiences

It is really important to be clear about who is being targeted by any promotional literature that you are commissioned to write, and this is also true for press releases. Ask your client who they hope to reach with their news story. Are you writing for publications that reach the right audience, and are you writing in an appropriate style? It is always important to be clear and concise in a press release, but there is still scope to use longer words for an academic subject, and more slang if the press release will go to teen magazines or websites.

Sending a release

If you have good contacts in the media already, you may want to offer to send press releases as well as write them. Larger companies subscribe to databases of contacts which can help finding the right person to contact. However, if you are a sole trader it can be more cost effective to buy the publication you want to target, or

---

Press release

Issued Date......

For immediate release OR embargoed until Date......

Title . . . make it brief and attention-grabbing

The first sentence should be a summary of the story. Get your key points across to catch the journalist's attention or they may not read further. Answer all the important questions like who, what, where, when, why and how. Write as if you are speaking to the readers of the publication – review your target publication for an appropriate style.

Expand on the details in the second paragraph. Remember the journalist will want to know what is unique or new about your story and why it will appeal to their readers. Then back up your claims with facts and statistics in the following paragraphs. Write in the present tense, and use 'he' or 'she' instead of 'I'.

Go on to illustrate your story with quotes. *'A quote, written in italics, from a key person, helps bring a story to life. Make sure your quote adds new information to the release.'*

As well as quotes, you could use bullet points to highlight points about your story:

· Special
· Timely
· Unique.

Finish off with details such as dates, times, how to order or contact you – this only needs to be brief, and should be the details you would like to see in print. Fuller details can go in 'Notes to editors', below.

##Ends##

More/over

Notes to editors
1. *Tell the editor who to contact for more information – include mobile, landline and email if possible.*
2. *Also include short background information on the company, when it was launched, achievements, mini biography of the founder, etc.*
3. *Include the company name, fax number, email and website address.*
4. *Include opening hours, prices, venues, dates as appropriate to the story.*
5. *State whether there are photographs available.*

167

simply call to ask who you should speak to.

Plan carefully before calling journalists. Be clear about what you have to offer, and how it could fit with their page or programme. Have the press release available, and be ready to amend it if necessary to answer any questions they may raise during your discussion. Think about your opening question too. You may want to start by finding out whether they are free to talk, and, if not, ask when would be best to call back. That way you avoid trying to get their attention when they have an imminent deadline.

Most releases go by email today. Never attach a press release file to an email as it increases the chance that it will get deleted by spam filters, and you are relying on the journalist to click and open the file. You will probably want to include a small, low resolution image. A picture can really sell a story. Don't send lots of high resolution images, as they will fill up the recipient's inbox. Simply state that in the editor's notes 'hi res' images are available.

There are times when you will want to print press releases. Use A4 paper with a logo header, and number the pages. Use only one side of the paper. Press releases can accompany samples, or form part of a larger 'media pack'.

Writing for a media pack

There is plenty of scope for writing to form part of a company's media pack. A media pack may be handed out to journalists attending shows or exhibitions, sent out to enquirers, or mailed proactively as part of a PR campaign. A conventional media pack is continued in an A4 folder, although a more imaginative approach may catch a greater number of journalists' attention. You can also turn a media pack into a goody bag, with space for samples and 'pillow gifts'. Pillow gifts could include chocolates, drinks, or other useful items to encourage journalists to cover the story. You may arrange for company branding or the product image or name to be included on these gifts. This approach is suitable for events and consumer products and services. Think carefully about the target audience for your media pack and make sure that any extras are well targeted.

A media pack could include:

- recent press release(s);
- photographs or high-resolution images on a disc;
- samples;
- a company biography;
- feature ideas or tips.

Every item in the media pack should have press contact details. This is straightforward for printed paper, but you may need to add stickers to samples and the back of photographs. Read on for specifics on how to write a couple of possible inclusions.

Company biography
For media purposes, a company biography needs to be clear and concise. Include essential dates such as when the company was founded. Supply quotes from key people in the company, and make sure that the people and quotes are relevant to the current activities, products or events you are promoting. Use headed paper, and small images of people and places that are important to the story. If the company founder has a good story of how he or she started, this would be worth including. If the company has been nominated or shortlisted for or has won any recent awards, mention this too.

Avoid unnecessary detail. Once you have written a company biography stand back and try to reread it with an impartial eye. While the company owner may want everyone to know the names and ages of his or her dogs, for most purposes this will be superfluous. Of course, if you are going to be contacting canine media or are promoting doggy products this information will be of greater interest, so knowing the target audience can make it easier to perfect the company information.

Alongside the usual contact details, you should mention who at the company is available for comment on different subjects, and if there is a specific contact to set up an interview.

Tips and feature ideas

If you are distributing media packs to journalists you want to encourage them to include the company's products or services in as many ways as possible. You may be asked to come up with some feature ideas to include on a sheet in the media pack. If the company you are writing for has a new personal service, it is easy to include an invitation for a journalist to try it. Alternatively, there may be potential for a reader trial.

You might also be requested to write up some relevant tips. When included in a media pack this sort of 'mini feature' is available for journalists to include in their own article. Local publications may print the tips in their entirety. You need to come up with tips that have a broad relevance and may improve the use or understanding of something relevant to the company you are writing for. For example, if you are working on a promotion for a lunchbox snack, you could write five tips for parents on how to create a healthy packed lunch. Any mention of a specific product in these tips should be clear yet low key. The emphasis should be on providing good information rather than an advertisement. Do some research, as you would for writing a feature or book, to ensure that the tip content is original and accurate. The more inspiring and relevant the tips, the more likely they are to be used, and the more likely the company is to get you writing for them again.

Get some experience

Proven experience in PR will help you get clients, but how do you get started? Why not offer your services to a local charity? If they have an event coming up you can practise by writing a press release and calling the local media to tell them what's going on. Keep a record of the press release and any supporting materials you created, together with cuttings of any coverage you generated. You might know someone who runs a small business who would be grateful if you did some PR work for them which you could add to your examples of work too. Fiona says, 'When I started I wanted a website, but didn't have the money to spare. I linked up with a new web designer. She designed a site for me, and I did some work promoting her business. It helped each of us get more work in our portfolio and generate new clients.'

Steve McComish started his professional life as a journalist. He says,

I spent around twelve years as a journalist, including five as the *Daily Mirror* Midlands correspondent. I took the NCTJ course. I think it is a brilliant training, and work on a local paper is a good training ground for writing of any kind. Every day I had to come up with two page leads of 400 words, plus around ten shorter articles and maybe twenty nibs. The NCTJ course gave me the broad general knowledge I needed, and now I work in PR I know what journalists need to know. Most press releases go straight in the bin. When I was a journalist I'd throw out nine out of ten. But they need news, and you need to send them stuff that is relevant to their readers. What is relevant to the person reading the paper isn't always the same as what seems relevant to the business owner: as a PR person you need to point that out. Basically, you need to learn 'news sense'. I think my press skills give me an edge over someone with just a marketing background. So many marketers do great pitches and presentations, but wouldn't know a good story if it hit them between the eyes.

Professional organizations and training providers

Join a professional body
If you would like to learn more about public relations, there are a number of professional bodies and training providers that can help. It is not compulsory to be a member of a professional body, but it will give clients confidence, and you can access ongoing training.

The Chartered Institute of Public Relations is one of two professional bodies for the industry, and the most relevant one for individuals. Membership costs a couple of hundred pounds a year and gives you access to reduced rates for courses leading to PR qualifications and relevant ongoing training. There are different levels of membership according to your level of experience. To find out more visit www.cipr.co.uk, call 020 7766 3333 or email membership@cipr.co.uk. The Public Relations Consultancy Association is the other professional body for the industry. Its membership is made up of public relations consultancies in the UK, and you need at least one year in trading and three employees to join.

Tracey Dooley of MediaMinister.co.uk took a Diploma in Public Relations with the London School of Public Relations just after she graduated. She says:

> This was a fairly intensive course, and there was a *lot* to take in. But it was immensely comprehensive and useful, not least because it led very quickly to a job in PR. I reckon I still use some if not most of the principles taught, and it has since certainly helped provide a launch pad to numerous related career paths.

For reading matter, subscribe to *PR Week*, which covers corporate and voluntary sector PR. CIPR members receive the magazine as part of their subscription.

Getting work

Decide whether you are looking for freelance work for a large organization or whether you want to offer small businesses help with their PR.

Freelancing for an agency
A PR agency or the PR department of an organization is likely to want help at busy times, when they are doing some focused promotion for a client or running an event. They will be looking for someone with good organizational skills too, who doesn't mind picking up the telephone and has a friendly and persuasive

manner. You could be involved in arranging venues and catering, and calling round key people in the media to persuade them to attend the events. At an event you might look after everything that the journalists attending need on the day, and send on any further information on the product after the event. This could mean taking some standard information or a prepared press release and rewriting it or adding extra information or images to answer their queries.

You need to put together a CV with details of your experience, and find contacts for the head of communications or public relations at relevant businesses. You might also want to approach charities, many of whom have a PR office, and public organizations such as your local council.

Local contacts

Alternatively, approach local companies with details of how you can help them. You should have a portfolio of work prepared, and ideally a website to direct people to. You should come up with a few key reasons why you can help their company, and the benefits of working with you. Make a list of potential clients and draft a letter or email highlighting how your skills can solve their problems. For a small business, the owner may be looking for a few hours of your time to come up with a press release based on his or her idea. Alternatively, they may want you to look at the business and work out some newsworthy ideas to promote.

Getting in touch

For PR agencies, businesses or any organization, it is far more effective to contact a named person than writing to 'The Director' or another job title. Make a few calls to find who is in charge of hiring outside help, and address the letter or email to them. Once you have sent your letter or email, think about contacting the addressee after a few days. It will help to script out your call, and work out possible questions they may have for you so you have well-thought-out answers all ready.

PR and networking

At the same time as promoting your business directly to companies, think about doing a little PR for yourself. How can you make contact with local businesses and build your reputation so that they are coming to you asking for help? Logically, you may want to talk to the local newspaper. It will help you build relationships with the journalists there, and you may get some coverage for your new business. Join networking groups too. There are usually groups meeting for breakfast, lunchtime talks or drinks after work. Look up the chamber of commerce in your area to get started. Most areas have an enterprise agency, which can be a good source of local business contacts. You could make up some flyers promoting your PR services and see if you can distribute them to networking groups and the enterprise agency.

Set up a website

A website is an excellent way to show what you have on offer. You can direct people to it in an email or letter, if they want to find out more about your service. You can spend as little as £30 getting a basic 'website in a box' online or from a computer store and customize it yourself, or find a web designer to set up something simple for you for a few hundred pounds.

Get some examples of your work on the site. You should aim to have clippings of news coverage that has resulted from your press releases as well as the releases themselves to convince potential clients that your writing and other PR skills generate results. You may also want to have some persuasive text highlighting how PR can help their company. Think about the terms people might search on and include this in your text too.

Get your website listed on local directories and business listings. Swap links with websites for complementary businesses offering business-to-business services.

Setting your rates

You will need to think about how much to charge for your work. The NUJ's London Freelance branch has an invaluable 'Rate for the Job' guide which shows how much members have been paid for work. Look at the 'shifts' rates for day rates for PR work: www.londonfreelance.org/rates. You may also want to check out competitors' websites or call round other companies to find out about their rates to ensure you are competitive. It can be difficult to get your rates right when you are starting out and need to generate business. Beware of setting your rates too low, as it can be hard to put them up later. If you set them and find potential clients wavering because of the cost, remember that you have the option to offer a discount. The CIPR website has a template contract for members to download.

Linda Jones
Linda Jones is a director of Passionate Media, www.passionatemedia.co.uk. She started the company after realizing her career on a regional evening newspaper was not going to work after the birth of her twin daughters. She says, 'I knew if I carried on I could never see the kids, so I decided on a different approach.' Linda learnt about PR after she first went freelance. She says:

> I worked with a PR agency in Birmingham, and saw how I could start a PR business. I set up Passionate Media, and have built a team of five other women, all of whom work part time. We do PR for a local hospice and for a local optician's practice, among other small businesses. We might be able to make more money by doing more one-off press releases, but we prefer to develop relationships with clients.

Passionate Media also offers media training for local businesses, working with community groups on press releases and training local government staff in media relations, for example. Linda says, 'This is a well-paying part of our work.'

Linda's team of five include an office manager who handles the admin, and can also turn her hand to sending press releases. Two team members focus on copywriting and PR, while Linda's co-director Carol Garrington is the marketing director. Linda says, 'Being part of a team means that I still have time for feature writing, which I enjoy, even if the PR pays better.'

One of the most important elements of running a successful

company is Linda's business knowledge. She says, 'I take advantage of whatever courses are being run by the local chamber of commerce or Business Link. I invest time in these events and listening to advisers. I have ongoing mentoring from a business adviser. We talk about the targets and goals for Passionate Media. He even has us filling in time sheets.' Linda spends much of her time doing marketing, networking and training. She says:

> I have worked very hard to build the company, make sure the office procedures are there, and holiday issues function 100 per cent. Running my own business gives me the flexibility to meet my daughters from school, or stay home when one of them is sick, but this has to be balanced with reasonable expectations about what I take out financially. Fortunately, as the kids get older I have more hours to put into the company and can see my income grow too.

Linda's tip if you want to work in PR is, 'Look at meeting the needs of journalists. You need to have a reality check and experience of what will work in the media. You have to deal with clients who make twenty changes to a press release so it reads like an advertorial. You can't be a yes-man, but must be able to tell them what will make news.' Linda adds, 'My biggest lesson is "don't compete on price", as you end up with clients who are looking for the cheapest rates. Compete on the calibre of what you offer, and back it up with testimonials and examples.'

PR potential?

So, are you ready to make a career in PR? Before you get started, ask yourself:

- Do I have relevant experience and skills, or how can I get some PR practice and training?
- Who do I want to target with my PR service?
- Am I clear about what I can offer and my rates?
- How will I reach potential clients?

Make an action plan to help you resolve any issues raised by these questions and you will soon be ready to start making a living in PR.

Chapter 9

Journalism

If you want to write for a living, journalism can be an exciting sector to aim for. However, it is competitive to break into, the hours can be long and antisocial, and the pay is extremely variable. For every freelancer making a good living, there are several more struggling to get their pitches accepted, and many turn to other jobs to pay the bills. However, if nothing beats the feeling of seeing your work in print and you have the determination to persist, journalism is a fascinating and worthwhile occupation.

There are three different areas of written journalism, and this chapter will focus on writing for newspapers and magazines. Read Chapter 10 to find out about online journalism, which is of growing importance.

What the job involves

Newspapers
If you work on a newspaper, you will have a varied and busy job. You may be interviewing a bereaved relative in the morning and a local councillor or an MP in the afternoon. Throughout the day you will be receiving calls, emails and press releases. Some of these will be unsolicited, from those with something to promote, real people

178

with a story, or from your contacts. Building up contacts is a key to success. If you have someone in the know at the local council, at key organizations, in the police or at the local hospital, it will ensure you get to hear about important stories first. You may need to follow up the information these contacts have given you and do your own independent research to check things out. Stories can also come out of events, meetings and conferences which you would need to attend. At times you may need to take the newsdesk phone calls and follow up the leads that come in, working closely with other members of the news team, photographers and editors.

You will need to be able to write accurate and concise copy in the style of the paper, and to meet deadlines every time. You may find that the story you have carefully researched and crafted suddenly gets moved or dropped, as other more compelling and timely news comes in. Alongside longer and more in-depth stories, most newspaper journalists will also be supplying a number of shorter fillers and 'nibs'. It is likely that you will also be responsible for creating content for the newspaper website and uploading it.

Sarah Lewis
Sarah Lewis started out writing freelance for a Brighton magazine called *Insight*. She says:

> If you want to get into writing for local magazines, many are cash strapped and will bite your hand off if you will do something for free. It can be hard to then make the move to paid writing, but most will have a small budget. I wrote one or two articles for free, then when it became more regular asked for payment, with success.

When *Insight* closed, Sarah launched a magazine called *Rocks*, aimed at Brighton's alternative community. She says:

> I was printing it on the local paper's press, and after a few months they started showing an interest. *Rocks* was bought out by *Newsquest* and I continued as editor. I also become the *Argus*'s environmental reporter and won the EDF Energy Environmental Journalist of the Year award. Sadly, the magazine was closed after eighteen months.

I was made redundant and now write freelance for the *Argus*.

I've written for pretty much every publication in Brighton. You can be hard pressed to make a living writing for local publications. You may only get £50 for something that could earn you hundreds of pounds if it was in a national paper, yet you still have to put in the same time and research. I know plenty of journalists who back up their freelance income by offering complementary therapies, taking in lodgers, doing photography or writing books.

If you want to write for local newspapers, Sarah advises:

Find out who runs the news desk or features desk. Give them a call to introduce yourself and ask about the sort of ideas they are after: you can pitch over the phone or follow up with an idea by email. You just need to persist. When I was editing *Rocks* I would tell new or work experience people to nag me because emails or ideas can get so easily lost in the hectic day-to-day running of a mag or paper. It's really easy to feel demotivated when things don't go the right way but the people who succeed are the people who keep on going regardless.

Magazines

If you want to write for a magazine, you may think of glossy high-profile news-stand titles, but there are thousands more magazines out there and the reality is that there is more work available for these specialist business and trade titles.

There are many similarities between work on a newspaper and work on a magazine. In both, a journalist will research and write news and features, but the length and style of the articles will differ, as will the timescales. Whatever sort of publication you are writing for, you will need to understand the readers and what interests them. On a magazine you may work mainly on features in a particular area, or be responsible for news. You will need to gather press releases, make contacts and attend events as a way of gathering new ideas and stories. You may get together on a regular basis with the magazine or section editor to plan out the stories for one or more issues, and allocate work. If you are working on a freelance basis you will send in stories to the commissioning editor. If he or she likes them he or she will slot them in and commission you.

Sub-editing

Some journalists work as sub-editors on national, regional and local newspapers and magazines. A 'sub' goes through all the copy prior to publication and checks its accuracy, tone and style. You might also be called upon to have knowledge of the law, so you can pick up potential problems before the paper goes to press. You may simply need to remove spelling mistakes or grammatical errors, cut to fit a space, or rewrite and expand whole sections. As a result you won't simply be working at a computer; you will also be calling up journalists to check facts and ask for amendments or extra material, and liaising with an editor if you have concerns. Some subs will compile regular features, such as sports results tables.

The sub will also need to devise relevant headlines and write 'stand firsts', the introduction to a story. A sub will work on the layout of the paper and page design, fitting in photos and writing captions. There will probably be an element of proofreading too (see Chapter 11). This is a job where an eye for detail is vital, alongside the ability to work under pressure to meet regular deadlines.

Emma Cooper
Emma Cooper has been editing for fifteen years. She says:

> My first job was as an editorial assistant/junior writer on a monthly journal which provided information about EU legislation to local authorities. I soon learned how to mark up copy using British Standard proof correction marks and gained a good understanding of the processes involved in preparing a document for publication. I learned most of my skills on the job, but I did attend a couple of useful training courses at the Publishing Training Centre in Wandsworth.

Emma now runs her own business, Amberweb. She offers a range of services. Emma says:

> I do copy-editing (also known as sub-editing) for magazines, training materials, corporate communications, promotional materials, websites and all sorts of publications. This involves checking the author's original text to make sure it flows well, is error-free, grammatically correct and consistent throughout before publication. A copy-editor would also double-check basic facts such as web addresses, company names and dates, and also check that the publication is accurately referenced in terms of headings, cross-references, etc. Any outstanding queries or ambiguities are sent back to the author/publisher for review. I also do proofreading, which involves carrying out a final quality check of a document (after it has been typeset or formatted for online use) prior to publication.

If you want to become a sub-editor, Emma advises:

> It goes without saying that you need to have a good knowledge of spelling, grammar and punctuation. Decent writing skills are also essential, as you are often required to do a certain amount of rewriting. A wide general knowledge is useful, so you can spot any glaring factual errors. You also need to be well organized – as a freelancer I am often working on several projects at one time. Finally, you need good computer skills, as I am increasingly being asked to edit on-screen rather than the traditional method of marking up hard copy.

Personality

A newspaper or magazine journalist needs to be interested in an enormous range of subjects, people and events: if you are working freelance your ability to carve out a range of niches can mean success or failure. A journalist needs to be inquisitive, eager to follow up ideas and turn them into stories.

You need to be able to see the broad picture, have the persistence and intelligence to research a subject and have an eye for detail, especially when checking your final draft. Whether freelance or staff, you need to be able to work well under pressure, cope with irregular hours and react well to stress. As a freelance you have the additional pressure of ensuring that you earn enough to pay the bills. Journalism rarely pays brilliantly, so material girls and boys should probably look at PR instead.

Writing style

The style of writing will depend on the publication you are working for and the slot that you fill in that publication. It can help if your written style is easy to understand and, of course, you have excellent spelling, grammar and punctuation.

If you want to break into a writing career, Patricia, who has been writing for around twenty-three years, advises that you need:

The ability to be able to bullshit. Really. You have to be able to say something about anything, even something that bores you rigid or about which you know nothing. And you have to be able to apply yourself – like many jobs, it is very often a slog and you can't expect to have fun all the time, or even most of the time. You need persistence, and a thick skin. As a writer you can't afford to take rejection personally. Be honest: don't pretend to know about a subject if you don't. You have to allow the people you're interviewing to help you out. If you want to do well in journalism, learn proper feature construction, and news construction. Learn how to spell. Don't think you're Henry James and that people actually want to read you – journalism is not creative writing. And get your copy in on time. So many people don't. I am a witch for deadlines because I spent so long in production and suffered so much when writers were late. The truth is, journalism isn't rocket science: if you can produce literate, readable copy, on time, that ticks all the boxes, you can actually get away with being quite a mediocre writer because the subs will rewrite it all anyway. But a great writer who's unreliable and late is no use to anyone. There are too many people in this profession who think they're Hunter S. Thompson and they're not.'

Skills

Pitching

If you can master pitching, you are more likely to succeed as a freelancer. A pitch is a short paragraph that you send to a commissioning editor, outlining your idea for an article and why you are ideally placed to write it. Alternatively, you can pitch over the phone.

Having the idea might be the hardest part, or it may come easily to you. If you are lacking inspiration, read widely, listen to the media, browse news sites on the net and talk to people. You never know where inspiration might come from. Keep a file of ideas to go back to if you have more than you can deal with.

Freelancer Sarah Ewing doesn't set aside a rigid time to send out pitches, but does it as she has an idea. She says:

> If I see something that leads to an idea I'll email it off right away. I may spend two hours a week pitching in total. Sometimes one of the editors I work for on a regular basis may say that she has a features meeting coming up, and ask me to contribute ideas, and then I'll spend half an hour brainstorming, but I think my best ideas come when I least expect them.

Freelance writer Patricia has plenty of experience at coming up with ideas for features. She says:

> For things that interest me, I am always full of ideas, so that's no problem – but that's years of practice at having to come up with stuff! When you're on a weekly, with a slot to fill, you can't mess about with writer's block. If I was in a slump when writing about property, France, etc., I'd scour the French magazines to see what they're writing about, then work up something similar for the English market. I'm a member of forums and log on to RSS feeds,

etc., of course. The problem really is having too many ideas, rather than not having enough.

Patricia's big downside for working as a journalist is pitching. She explains, 'It can be soul-destroying, particularly when you find great subjects that no one wants to publish. I also hate it when people want pictures for free or argue with your rates. To be honest, PR work is often easier and the people are nicer and more grateful.'

Before you pitch, study the publication you are aiming at. Make sure you can see how your proposal might fit in with their pages, and check that they haven't covered a similar story. You should also be aware of what competing magazines are covering, as publications won't want to include a feature on a similar topic to a competitor's latest issue. You should also find out who commissions articles. Call up the editorial assistant to find out, if you are unsure.

Sarah Ewing explains how she got into writing celeb stories:

I was approached by *Healthy* to write some pure health features about three years ago. Then the editor asked me if I could write a celeb interview that they had booked with Nell McAndrew. Nell liked it and the editor did too, and after that I got a regular slot to write their celeb covers. With the *Sunday Express*, I identified two celeb slots where the same sort of celebrities that I get offered for *Healthy* would work well. I now find I can quite easily place a short Q&A with a celeb as well as a longer interview.

When making a pitch, you can either phone or email. A phone call has the advantage of immediate feedback, but may interrupt the commissioning editor at a time when he or she is busy, cutting your chances of a positive response. An initial email outlining your idea in a couple of lines can give him or her the chance to respond when it suits. However, it is highly likely that you will send out pitches and then hear nothing. Leave it a few days then do get on the phone. It is much better to find out for certain that the magazine is not interested. You might get more detailed feedback that will help you make a more successful pitch next time: 'We're really looking for stories about younger women than that.' Getting a firm no also mean that you are free to pitch the feature elsewhere. Some journalists do pitch an idea to more than one publication at a time, but before doing that you need to consider what you would do if two or more said yes.

Liat Joshi has a few suggestions for key skills that any freelance journalist will need:

> Be able to market yourself and to recognize what editors want for their publication. You need tenacity if you want to be a freelance journalist. You've got to chase, chase and chase those editors to get commissions. And that's just the ones who know your name. Add a few more chases for the ones who don't know you. You should also be able to cope with a fairly solitary working day.

Negotiating skills
Once you have a yes, your best bet is to ask the commissioning editor to name a price to use your article in the publication. It is not always easy to get them to make an offer: look at the NUJ's 'Rate for the Job' website http://media.gn.apc.org/feesguide/index. html to see what other freelancers have earned. The NUJ advise asking for at least a third more than quoted on this site. Research the publisher and find out the size of their operation too. The more work you do, the more of a feel you will get for an acceptable fee. If you get a low offer, you don't have to accept it: aim to negotiate it up. If you think you might be able to sell the idea elsewhere for more, you may even want to walk away at that point.

Once you have agreed a fee for first use, you can then ask whether the publication will want to use your work online or reprint it in another edition, and you should aim to negotiate a further fee, from 50 to 100 per cent, for each additional use.

Structuring your work
The structure of a piece of writing can get the reader interested and maintain that interest to the end. How you structure your copy will depend on the audience and the publication. Broadly,

though, you need to explain the story briefly in the introductory paragraph, and fill in details in subsequent ones. There may be highs and lows in a case study-based feature. In a news or factual piece, you may want to have several paragraphs introducing different viewpoints. And finally, for every piece there must be a conclusion or summary. As you develop your writing skills you will become more adept at identifying the structure of an article and outlining sections before you start writing. When reading magazines and newspapers, look at the work of different writers and see how they use the structure of a piece to get you interested and keep you reading until the end. Equally, if you are reading something and find your interest wavering, ask yourself why.

Contacts and case studies

Any journalist needs to be good with people. You will need to develop a good range of contacts. Contacts may work at useful organizations or have specialist knowledge. Build up a selection of people who might be the source of a good story, and stay in touch with them on a regular basis, by email or at a quick coffee meeting. You need to look after your contacts: someone who has helped you in the past and had a good experience may be able to help again when you are looking for someone with a story to fit a feature you are writing.

If you can find good case studies, this can make life as a freelance journalist much easier. Many publications are interested in real-life stories, and it is real people who make news. There is no easy way to start off finding case studies: you need to build up your networks over time. Talk to people, email old friends and colleagues too. There are plenty of sites on the internet that link up journalists and would-be case studies, and Response Source, www.responsesource.com, which puts journalists in touch with PRs. Some journalists even run their own newsletter asking for help finding case studies for the stories that they are working on at the time. You may need to be persuasive to get some people to help you, and clear about exactly what they are in for, as many people are nervous of the media.

Interviews

Once you have found the people behind the story, you need to interview then. See below for tips on the technical side of recording an interview. Preparation is essential before most interviews. Know what you need to find out, and research your interviewee's background. Plan some good questions, but be prepared to follow where the conversation leads and you may find out things you did not even know to ask about. You need to find a balance between following your own agenda and that of the interviewee. Develop experience of interviewing face to face and over the phone. Freelancer Patricia advises, 'When you're interviewing people, learn to listen, not just talk. Get your questions sorted and make sure you cover them all, but listen to the replies and riff off of them – it's the strange byways you go down that are the most interesting. Most people are really keen to talk, if you will only let them talk and not keep interrupting them.'

Self-editing

Editing can be much more than checking for grammar, spelling and consistency, but that is a good place to start. As a would-be journalist, you need to be able to stand back and look at your work as the editor might see it. When going through your work, Emma Cooper of Amberweb advises:

> Make it easy for the reader. Cut down wordy sentences. Chop up long paragraphs. Use bullet lists where appropriate to break up the text. Try to avoid too much repetition. Get a good dictionary! Don't rely on the computer's spell checker – it will not pick up spelling mistakes which spell another word. Always double-check any foreign words you are using in your document.

Error-free copy can make an editor feel far more warmly about commissioning you again. You will also need to edit your work for length. Your reputation will be damaged if you consistently turn in work that is too long or too short. The editor has commissioned work to a certain length and that is what you should deliver.

Try tricks like reading your work aloud, or reading each paragraph or sentence out of context, to check that it makes sense and you have not missed out vital words. Become aware of the words that you overuse or misspell so you can check these extra carefully. Split overlong sentences into two if it makes the meaning clearer. Look at whether the words you are using are ones that the readers will understand, or whether you need to replace a long word with a couple of short ones.

Knowledge

Shorthand

As a journalist, do you need shorthand? Many journalists who have gone through a full training course will wonder how anyone could manage without it, and if you have a little time to invest it can really help when interviewing people, without the risks of background noise or technical problems associated with an audio recorder. It may give you an advantage when pitching for a job. Perhaps most importantly, it can enable you to take really detailed notes to back up a story in case of legal action: you want to make sure that any notes you make are clear and easy to find. A journalist experienced in shorthand can write between 80 and 120 words a minute, with practice. Choose between the more traditional Pitman shorthand, and Teeline, a newer system designed to be easier to learn and used by many journalists. You can buy 'teach yourself' books, like *Teeline for Journalists* by Dawn Johnston, or take a course, or you might find shorthand lessons included in journalism training.

Patricia says, 'I have been a journalist almost all my working life, though when I left university there was a recession, so I immediately went back to college to learn secretarial skills. After that I temped for a year, waiting to get into journalism. My secretarial training really helped in being a writer – shorthand and very fast typing were invaluable.'

Current affairs

In most situations, you will benefit from a good understanding of the way local and national government works. Even if you don't plan to cover council meetings for the local paper, you never know when there might be new legislation in your specialist area. You can find out about the relevant parliament or assembly at:

- UK Parliament at www.parliament.uk
- Scottish Parliament www.scottish.parliament.uk
- National Assembly for Wales www.assemblywales.org
- Northern Ireland Assembly www.niassembly.gov.uk

The legal books mentioned in the next section can help you understand about the process of creating and implementing the law.

Law

If you write anything, you need to be aware of the legal consequences, and every writer will benefit from understanding copyright. You should understand about defamation and how reporting reputation-damaging lies can see you involved in a costly court case for defamation. You also need to understand what you can report and what is covered by laws on privacy and confidentiality. You may get information from someone who needs to keep their identity out of the press, and knowledge of the law can help you protect your source.

An understanding of the Data Protection Act and Freedom of Information Act can help you get access to information that organizations may prefer to conceal. There are also laws on reporting on government information, be it security or defence related, or about local decision-making or elections. You need to stay up to date with changes in how you can report on race, religion and terrorism.

Additionally, if you get work as a news reporter you need to know what you can and cannot report on, and how the criminal and civil courts work. The copy that you write could end up influencing the jury if it comes out mid-trial. You need to be aware that, while you may take notes, you may not use a tape recorder or take photographs, for example. There are different reporting restrictions for juveniles.

Frances Quinn, freelance journalist and author of *Law for Journalists*, says:

> Freelances often assume that they don't need to know about the law, because they can leave it to commissioning editors to make sure copy is legally OK, but that's both unprofessional and dangerous. As the writer, you'll often be the one who knows all the background to the story, and so the best placed to be aware of any potential legal problems that might not be immediately obvious to a commissioning editor. You really need to understand the law yourself, so that, if you think there's anything in a story that needs checking by a lawyer, you can warn the commissioning editor, and get it legalled. If you do get it wrong, the people or companies you've written about can sue you personally, though in practice they tend to go for the publisher, who's more likely to be able to pay substantial damages. But while that might let you off the financial hook, it can damage your professional reputation if the other side wins, and it won't do much for your relationship with the publishers either.
>
> Every journalist needs at least a basic understanding of the law on libel, contempt of court, privacy and breach of confidence. You don't have to be an expert – that's what lawyers are for – but you need to know when there's a question to be asked. It's important to realize that the law doesn't just operate to stop you publishing information, it can be a help too. If you know your libel law, for example, you can write the story that someone wants to suppress, but do it in such a way that you're covered by a legal defence; if you understand the Data Protection Act, you can prevent people misusing it to deny you information (which happens a lot); and if you get to know the Freedom of Information Act, you can get access to tons of public information that's the key to some fantastic stories. The law can be your friend, if you know how to use it.

Business journalists also need to have a knowledge of the laws on confidentiality and how this might apply to materials that you work on. Laws on libel, privacy and breach of confidence can also be important. Quinn continues:

People often think that it's only tabloid journalists writing about the rich and famous who run the risk of breaking the law by what they write, but in fact writing about, or for, business, carries risks too. Companies can sue for libel if you write something that affects their reputation, and you can also be sued for malicious falsehood, if you publish something that's not true, and which causes the subject financial loss – and that could be as little as saying that a business-man is retiring when he isn't, and not making proper checks to ensure the story is true. Another risk people often aren't aware of is that if you publish leaked material, you could be liable for breach of confidence. This in itself could lead to heavy damages, but in addi-tion the company can try to force you to reveal your source. As a journalist, you're ethically bound not to do so but, if you refuse, you can be sent to prison.

If you're writing about business, you're dealing with people who can afford the very best lawyers, and they can and will sue. So it's essential that you know how to stay on the right side of the law.

This book is not a legal guide: any writer should sign up for a course like the NCTJ's distance learning course in media law, and have up-to-date texts to refer to. Law is different in Scotland, and there are some differences in Northern Ireland too which are highlighted in *McNae's Essential Law for Journalists*. Legislation is constantly updated, so update your reference books and visit the website accompanying *Law for Journalists*, www.pearsoned.co. uk/practicaljournalism, which has discussion questions and updates on major legal changes.

Essential legal reading:

* *McNae's Essential Law for Journalists*, Tom Welsh, Walter Greenwood and David Banks (OUP, 2007).
* *Scots Law for Journalists*, Alistair J. Bonnington and Rosalind McInnes (Green, 2009).
* *Law for Journalists*, Frances Quinn (Pearson, 2007).

Equipment

A working journalist needs to be able to record interviews and meetings. You may use shorthand (see above), but most people also own recording equipment. A digital recorder is an affordable option that, used correctly, can give excellent recording quality. Pay attention to the factors that improve the sound quality of your recordings as this can mean the difference between an excellent piece and the embarrassment of having to call your interviewee back to check inaudible details. You may want to make written notes of key points, or even have two recorders running if an interview is going to be irreplaceable. Always check your equipment is charged and functioning before you start.

Recording face-to-face interviews
An external microphone can make a big difference in a face-to-face interview. You could opt for a tie-clip, lapel, noise-cancelling or directional microphone. Lapel or tie-clip mics may pick up rustling noises from clothing. Omni-directional microphones can be used in interview situations but need a quiet environment. A handheld directional microphone is ideal for 'street' recording situations where you can hold it up to your interviewee's mouth.

Recording telephone interviews
You may also want an interceptor to plug in between your phone and the recorder to take down telephone interviews. Simply putting your phone on to speakerphone may lead to a recording full of hiss, background noise and echo: try it out before the interview. There are dedicated telephone recording systems and online services that offer to record conference and video calls to a digital sound file.

Cheryl Rickman started her writing career back in 1995, writing a column for a local newspaper and contributing to the student magazine. She says:

> I was beginning to build up a portfolio, sometimes writing for free or for a very small fee. However, I then began writing regular

freelance articles for *Better Business* magazine in 2000, which was the year I also set up my web writing business, so I've been professionally writing for eight years. I've been editor and interview writer for ilikemusic.com since 2001.

Experience

Staff jobs or freelance

As with many of the media sectors covered in this book, it is entirely possible to start as a freelance without ever having worked on the staff of a newspaper or magazine. However, a staff job will teach you how a publication works and allow you to learn key skills and make contacts. Read how two journalists got started in very different ways.

Sarah Ewing

Sarah Ewing always intended to write for a living, although she spent a brief period training to be a doctor before realizing she didn't like blood. She says:

> I then went on to do a post-graduate degree in journalism. I was in the US at the time, and decided to move back to the UK for work. I didn't have any media contacts, so checked out which temp agencies placed people in the media. I was fortunate enough to have a job at IPC within ten days of arriving back in the UK, working as PA to the editor of *Country Life*. I had no long-term plans to be a PA, and the magazine didn't even let junior staff write, but I got to know all about how the magazine worked. Even more importantly, I got to know when other vacancies were coming up. I spent time on *Ideal Home* and *Living* etc., each time in a PA role but with increasing responsibilities, such as co-ordinating photo shoots. Finally I moved to a features editor role, doing maternity cover at *Practical Parenting*.

When a magazine she was working for was sold to new owners, Sarah decided to go freelance. She says:

This was possibly about eighteen months earlier than would have been the ideal time to go freelance, but in many ways it was good to go freelance before a lot of my friends and peers. Many of them waited until they were on maternity leave to make the move and it is a lot harder to establish yourself as a freelance, forge new contacts and put in the hours you need if you are juggling work and a baby.

Sarah spent eighteen months building up her portfolio, writing for smaller newspapers and websites. She then started pitching to women's magazines. She says, 'My first piece in *Essentials*, five years ago, was a huge thing for me.' Now, Sarah writes around eight articles each month. She covers health, parenting and celebrity features and still does some news writing. She advises:

A lot of freelancers find one good patch, build a good relationship with one magazine, but would struggle if the editor moved on. I know a range of magazines will publish the features I write, and I'm probably emailing back and forth to around ten editors at any one time. When *First* went bust I panicked initially as they were contributing around 25 per cent of my income, but in reality all the celeb-based features could be redistributed, and now the editor from *First* is working at *Fabulous*.

Sarah has found that a businesslike approach to freelancing has helped her succeed. She explains, 'I set myself goals. Each year I create a spreadsheet of the magazines I write for and note down when I write the feature and the fee I achieve. At the end of the year I look back and set myself targets for the following year. If I've had one article in *Vogue*, I may aim for four.'

Liat Joshi

Liat Joshi has been writing on travel and parenting as a freelance journalist for five years. She explains how she started writing:

It sounds clichéd but writing was something I always wanted to do. I'd got sucked into working in the City as a management consultant. It was probably the lure of the money. When I finally came to and realized that a fat salary didn't mean much if you were working sixty-hour weeks, writing was the obvious direction to go in. I had actually written for the university newspaper, had a short piece in the *Manchester Evening News* and run some business writing courses so I wasn't a complete beginner.

Liat took a short course in freelance journalism at the City Lit in London, and then plunged in at the deep end. She says:

I did the pitch to the *Sunday Times* about halfway through the course. I picked it because I was a regular reader, felt my writing style fitted with theirs and because I had a story which I thought would work well for their Home section. I also thought I didn't really have anything to lose by approaching them. The worst thing that could happen would be that they could say no, or just ignore my emails – a pretty common occurrence in freelance journalism. The piece was about how I'd sold my house to a friend – how the friendship affected the sale process and how the sale process affected the friendship. They seemed very happy with it so I then sent a second pitch and they accepted that. From then on they started asking me to do pieces – all for the Home section – on a fairly regular basis. I did a mix of reviewing swanky interior-designed homes and stories about practical aspects of home-buying, selling and ownership. I also did a piece I proposed to them for the News Review section. Having this experience with the ST was like a badge of approval when I approached other publications. I was able to send editors links to my work on the ST website. I then wrote pieces for the *Guardian*, *Independent* and several magazines, before diversifying into books. One of my main tips would be to start writing about something you know well – a topic you have unique knowledge of if possible. An editor on one of the major publications needs quite a compelling reason to hire an 'unknown' writer. It's a risk for them.

Professional organizations and training providers

As a journalist, you should consider joining the National Union of Journalists. It is open to staff and freelancers, editors, photographers and public relations professionals as well as journalists. The NUJ campaigns on professional issues including rates of pay and overtime. Perhaps one of the biggest incentives for you to join is the way that the union will advise you on freelance fees, contracts and copyright, and will help you if clients aren't paying up on time. You can get help if you are experiencing bullying, or if your employer is neglecting your rights. It can help you when you are feeling isolated and unsure where to turn. The regular meetings can put you in touch with others in the same situation, and help you keep up to date on relevant issues. Visit the website, www.nuj.org.uk, or call 020 7278 7916 to find out more about membership. The NUJ also offers a range of training courses, covering topics including an introduction to journalism, getting started as a freelance, and feature writing. For more details see www.nujtraining.org.uk.

Potential journalists may want to look into courses run by the National Council for the Training of Journalists (www.nctj.com), which accredits and delivers a range of training courses, and offers one of the best-recognized journalism qualifications, the National Certificate Examination. You can take NCTJ courses in newspaper and magazine journalism by distance learning as well as at thirty-nine accredited colleges across the UK. There are also short courses in essentials such as law.

The NCTJ also offers careers information and continuing professional development, information and research, publications and events.

Linda Jones
Linda Jones combines running a PR company with a successful career in journalism. She explains how she got started:

> I trained back in 1990 with the *Wolverhampton Express and Star*. By
> training on the job any illusions you have about the way of a writer

or reporter are shattered: you are made aware of the realities very quickly. I learnt all about sub-editing too. It gives you a certain work ethic too when you have to do twenty stories a day. It is not about the craft of writing, it is the story and how you tell it. It is producing stories that fit the need of the editor.

Linda now works freelance.

At the moment I'm working on writing features for magazines and newspapers. I am writing a feature for *Practical Parenting* and another for *Take a Break*. I have about six or seven pitches at various stages, mainly for real-life stories for national women's magazines. I take some lower-paid jobs because I know they won't take me long to do. If a feature only takes an hour I can easily write four in a day. Other jobs, like a real-life story, may pay thousands of pounds, but you have to work hard for the money.

Getting freelance work

When starting out as a freelance journalist, you may have already had some time in a staff job to build up contacts. Make the most of them, but remember that your relationship will change once you are no longer an employee. Former colleagues who have promised you work may continue to be helpful, but others may seem to forget you as soon as your leaving party is over. You will need to continue to network, online and face to face, and stay in touch with people as if you haven't spoken for a couple of years you have lost any advantage you might once have had.

If you already have a portfolio of work, start by building a website. You can use free services like Wordpress with a minimal technical knowledge to come up with a professional-looking site that showcases what you can offer. Editors will expect to be able to see your previous work before commissioning you, and a website makes this simple for them.

If you don't have previous experience as a journalist and want to start freelancing, you need to put your efforts into developing a portfolio. If you have taken a journalism course, you will have already written some articles. If you are currently on a course, try to get something published in the college newspaper: student journalism can be a good place to start. There are plenty of local magazines and websites that will welcome contributions but won't pay you. You may find it necessary to do a few features like this to build up your portfolio. At the same time, start looking around at a range of media, read each publication thoroughly, and develop ideas so you can start pitching. A specialist niche, using knowledge that others won't have, can help you get your first article accepted: you may have left accountancy in search of a complete change, but could find your knowledge useful when pitching to business magazines, for example.

Applying for work

Sometimes you may need to send in a CV, even as a freelancer. Make sure you have a one-page summary of your experience and qualifications, amending it each time you use it to ensure it is up to date and relevant to that job. Be extra careful when checking for spelling and grammar as errors are likely to damage your chances of success.

Making it work

Freelancing can be uncertain at times. Prepare yourself well by saving up, and cutting down unnecessary expenses. Many journalists have a second way of making money, either by working in a related sector like PR or using a former skill such as web design. Sarah Ewing has some advice about how to deal with the financial instability, and shows how being a freelancer can work out well:

> When I started, my mortgage was £1,000 a month, which was far from ideal, even if it did mean I had a foot on the property ladder. Try not to overcommit financially. I've moved to Edinburgh which has saved me substantially on housing costs, plus given a boost to my travel writing. I also get asked to do any celeb interviews that are coming up in Scotland. You may think that you should be making decent money as a freelancer, but it is not your money until it lands

in your bank account. I've even thought of using invoice financing to cover the time between completing the work and payment landing in my bank account. I try to spread my risk, however, by working in a range of sectors, and I think my goals help keep me focused. I'm now on a really good income, I was aiming for around £60k this year, although may only reach £55k after *First* went bust. If I was editing a magazine section I would probably only be earning £40 or £45k, and without the flexibility that I have.

You also need unending motivation, patience and persistence. You may have the best ideas in the world, but struggle to get them commissioned. Stick at it, as it can take just one break, perhaps finally finding the editor who really likes your ideas, to reach the turning point. Sarah Ewing says, 'I have been in journalism for ten years, freelance for the last seven, and I would say everything has really only fallen into place in the last eighteen months. I didn't think it would take that long. Now I know I can come up with good ideas that will get commissioned.'

Ready to write?

So, are you ready to make a career as a journalist? Before you get started ask yourself:

- Do I have relevant experience and skills? If not, plan how to get writing and pitching.
- What niche or specialism can I develop?
- Which publications will fit my ideas?
- Am I clear about what I can offer and my rates?

Make an action plan to help you resolve any issues raised by these questions and you will soon be ready to start making a living as a journalist.

Chapter 10

New media copywriting

Writing for new media is one of the fastest growing areas for copy-writers. Every company that develops a new website or blog needs content. And, with the way that search engines rank sites more highly if they are updated on a regular basis, there is a continuing need for fresh copy. However, writing for the web is a slightly different skill from writing for print media, and you will need to be aware of the different approach required. Web writing can also be poorly paid, so it may take some time to find more profitable clients.

The work

You can find work to suit a range of talents online. If you have a background in marketing, you might want to offer your services to companies looking for help with email or SMS (short message service) marketing or creating pay-per-click campaigns and other online advertising. There are opportunities to work for businesses wanting to promote themselves through blogging too, if you have the ability to come up with newsy items on a regular basis. Many companies run an e-newsletter, but struggle to create or edit the content and make the newsletter look good, which is another opportunity if you have writing or design skills. Lots of websites need feature content if you have journalism talents.

Writing style

Writing for the web requires a different approach from writing for print media. It is harder to read on screen than in print, so items need to be shorter. A page with 200 or 300 words in print can seem quite short: the same information online fills the screen and may lose readers. Bullet points can make a big difference to how easy something is to digest. With eight years' experience, Cheryl Rickman has plenty of knowledge of what makes good web copy, and the pitfalls you should avoid. Explaining the difference between web and print in more detail, she says:

> People don't read copy on websites in the same way they read in print. Most of us don't read word for word but scan web pages for bits of interest, which is one reason why key words and sentences highlighted in bold can work well online. That, plus the fact that it takes 20 per cent longer to read a web page than a printed page means that web copy needs to be clear, concise and compelling. Web users like lists and bullet points, but don't like large chunks of text or scrolling pages. In fact, they will click away to your competitors' sites quicker than you can say world-wide-web, if you don't get what you say and how you say it right online. Good web copy:
>
> - encourages web visitors to take the desired action (enquire, buy, click, read on or register);
> - improves credibility;
> - is useful to the reader; and
> - is search-engine friendly, enabling more targeted web traffic.

If you need a quick guide to some pitfalls in web writing, Cheryl recommends you avoid, 'Long paragraphs and chunks of text, typos, and text copied from an offline printed brochure straight on to a website: it needs to be written for the web with shorter paragraphs in a more compelling quick-to-read fashion.'

You should also think about the words you are using. Shorter words are usually better than longer ones, to ensure maximum readability. Talk to the site's owner about the sort of keywords people use to search for the site, and see if you can incorporate relevant words in a natural way. To sum up, you can't beat the advice from freelance web writer Nancy Duin: 'Forget Henry James and embrace Ernest Hemingway! Strip your writing of all inessentials but not of humanity and personality. Think strategically: what message are you conveying, to which audience?'

Personality

Web writing can be a solitary occupation when it comes to putting ideas on to your computer, but you still need to have good people skills. You may need to liaise with clients or interview people, just as you would in any other type of business writing. If you can cope with technical details you will be able to offer a wider range of web services: if not, you might want to link up with a web designer who you can ask for technical help and refer clients to when they want work that is beyond your skills.

Skills

Search-engine optimization
If you are writing for the web it is important to understand the part content plays in search-engine optimization (SEO). You should have an understanding of how to make the words you write get picked up by search engines. If you are more technically minded, you may also want to find out about metatags, part of the code behind a website. And anyone who writes for blogs should know about using tags, words to describe the entry in the blog so others can search for topics of interest.

When writing for a website, you should discuss with your client the words that people are searching on to find their site, and search phrases by which they would like to be found. You then need to be able to include these words and phrases in the copy, in a natural way. Cheryl Rickman says, 'In order to be search-engine friendly, web copy must be keyword rich (but still make sense to the reader), have clear headlines and page titles and be relevant to the target audience (and searcher).' Overuse of keywords can lead to the site being penalized in search rankings (how high it appears in the search results when people search on that term). The more specific a phrase you use, the better targeted your results will be: try 'business writing' or 'commercial copywriting' compared to simply 'writing'.

There are thousands of websites and blogs to help you brush up your SEO skills and stay in touch. SEO Book, www.seobook.com, is highly rated by many and has some free tools as well as a subscription service. Popular search engines are continually refining the way they work, so site rank can rise and fall. Up-to-date knowledge can help you make the most of this. Other sites can help you choose the words to include in your web copy. Use Google AdWords to generate keyword ideas. Simply type in the words you know that you want to use and it will come up with variations and similar phrases. It will also give you a relative idea of the popularity of different words and phrases and how often they are searched for. Google Trends, www.google.com/trends, allows you to compare what people have been searching for over time; BlogPulse Trends, www.blogpulse.com/trend, does the same for blogs.

Knowledge

Writing or editing web content
If you are writing content for a website, you need to think carefully about the structure of the site. Some clients may ask you to suggest a structure as part of the work you do. It is important to think carefully about clear and relevant page titles and page descriptions. The page you are writing for will affect the content you create. Cheryl Rickman says, 'The home page should tell the reader what's in it for them. Avoid "We do this" copy instead of "you can do this" copy. "About us" type copy should go on a specific "about us" page.'

Social networking

You need to have a good knowledge of the ever-changing world of digital media if you are writing for the web. A business's website is one of their marketing tools. If you are helping them with their site content, you may want to advise them to set up a MySpace or Facebook page, or possibly a Twitter feed, depending on their target audience. As well as benefiting your client's business, social networking sites like LinkedIn and Ecademy can help you find work, stay in touch with former colleagues and clients and promote your business. Learning about social networking sites is something that is best done online as the popularity of sites changes and new ones spring up. Start at Wikipedia for an up-to-date list of current top sites, and to find out how many users are registered on each. The site also gives you a brief idea of who is the target audience for each social networking site. Register for sites relevant to yourself and your clients and start using them: it is the only way to really understand how they work and how they can help you. Be careful to read the rules before you start using a networking site to promote your business, as different sites allow different amounts of promotion: some are set up very much for business and others do not allow business promotion at all.

Experience

Writing for the web has changed enormously over the last twenty years. If you want to break into this area, you should be able to show clients other websites you have written for. If you have no commercial web-writing experience, start writing your own blog, and contribute to other sites to help you develop an idea of what works well on the web. If you are thinking of pitching to a magazine site, read the site, find out about submission guidelines, and make sure you have some examples of other things you have written in the same sphere. Similarly, if you are approaching businesses to offer your services in improving their website content, or as a paid blogger, have relevant examples of similar work. Ideally, you should also be able to show the results you have achieved with other websites, and concrete details of the increased numbers of visitors to the clients' sites as a result.

Fiona says:

> I wrote some copy for the front page of the website belonging to a woman who makes wedding place cards. It was simple to look at the keywords people were searching on and incorporate them into some natural-sounding text, describing the benefits and services offered by the business. This made an enormous difference to the number of people ordering cards from the site, so much in fact that she asked me to write another section explaining about delivery times and the need to order well in advance of your wedding. The improved front page gave her business a real boost, and meant that she was working to capacity.

Have your own website which you regularly update with content that will interest potential clients, and which contains plenty of relevant keywords for when clients are searching to find someone to help them out. Make sure that you link to other sites you have written for, and include customer testimonials with links back to the client's website, which adds to a reader's confidence that the testimonials are genuine.

Professional organizations and training providers

The NUJ (www.nujtraining.org.uk) offers an introduction to online publishing and a course in writing for the web as well as more specific skills like podcasting, videoblogging and setting up a blog. The NCTJ (www.nctj.com) also runs a course in video and audio reporting for the web.

Staying in touch
Visit New Media Knowledge, www.nmk.co.uk, for articles, and events focused on digital media. It also promotes full-time and short courses from the University of Westminster, including those on working in computer gaming, an area requiring specialist writing skills. You could also subscribe to *New Media Age*,

www.nma.co.uk, a weekly magazine covering interactive media: the internet, wireless internet and interactive TV. *Revolution*, www.brandrepublic.com/revolution, is a new media magazine for marketers.

Getting work

As with any other area of writing, your success in generating work will depend on how you put the word out about your services. Think about the clients you want to target, and how you will reach them. If you want to help local businesses who have yet to create a web presence, you should probably contact them in writing, face to face or on the phone. A business without a website is likely to be run by someone who would prefer this more traditional approach. If, however, you are looking to get involved with digital and new media companies, you should approach them by email, and have your CV available electronically: a pdf is a format that can be read by most people. Also have a portfolio of your work online.

If you are looking for work, Nancy Duin advises:

> Get entries in as many relevant directories as possible. My main ones are the Society for Editors and Proofreaders (SfEP) (I get most of my work from that) and the NUJ, but am also in the Medical Journalists' Association one and the Society of Authors', plus other, general editorial ones. Tell all your friends and acquaintances that you have 'spare capacity'. Subscribe to newsletters/feeds and follow up even the most obscure leads. I read on the New Media Age daily bulletin that The History Channel's website was being redesigned by an agency. I got in touch with the agency's MD, whose name was given in the announcement. He passed my CV on to The History Channel and I eventually did some writing for them.

Look online for freelance writing directories and journalism job sites. There are plenty of them: see Chapter 4 for a list. Think about the specialist services you will offer: are you going to focus on writing newsletters, or use previous experience in an industry, such as financial services, and develop a niche there? Read on for more ideas about areas to work in towards the end of the chapter.

Cheryl Rickman has been writing for the web since 2000. She explains how she got started:

> After graduating with a very general media degree I worked as an editorial assistant in London, with my long-term ambition to work as an editor on a music magazine and/or work from home as a freelance writer. Commuting to London from Winchester wasn't that much fun, so I found a job as assistant editor/internet marketing executive closer to home. During this time I wrote two booklets on 'how to create a winning website' and 'how to promote your website successfully' which gave me the expertise/knowledge to start my own business appraising websites and providing a web copywriting service. After the company I worked for went bust, I launched forth and established WebCopywriter.co.uk. Alongside this I wrote business articles for *Better Business* magazine, and ran my business from home. I also work on ilikemusic.com as Editor, so my dreams and ambitions, to work as a music magazine editor and work from home as a freelance writer, both came true after a lot of hard work and persistence.

Writing for a client

There is plenty of work in devising web pages for business clients, small and large. Whichever sort of business you want to work with, you need to make some contacts. Attend business or media networking events and join relevant forums and email groups. Set up a website promoting your online copywriting, with links to sites that you have written for.

Online feature writing

Many magazine-type websites commission features in the same way as magazines. You will need to find the contact details for the company behind the site and ring up to get the name of the commissioning editor as the 'contact us' addresses on a site are unlikely to go to the right person. Remember that features need to be structured differently online. Keep the length down and break up blocks of text with lists and bullets.

Keris has written features for AllAboutYou.com. She says, 'These are a lot shorter than the magazine features, and the rate of pay isn't quite as good. I was getting around £150 for 700 words, compared to some magazines which were paying around £300 per thousand.'

Pay

There is an enormous difference in pay for online features, and some sites seem very much aimed at the enthusiastic amateur who has another source of income. Others have high demands to earn your wage: one site offers £9.25 per 400-word article, with a minimum requirement of a hundred articles a month. Another well-known web information provider takes on freelances to maintain a minisite in their specialist area. Your payment is based on the revenue generated from advertisements on your pages. After submitting an initial sample of your work, you may be selected to be 'in prep', or the preparation stage, where you create the site from scratch. However, this is all part of the application process, and you may put in considerable hours of work only to find you have not been hired. A number of websites pay based on the ad revenue generated by your content.

Nancy Duin
Nancy Duin has been writing freelance for around thirty years. Her web writing career almost happened by accident. She says:

> I was working as an editorial consultant for Channel 4 in programme support. We produced booklets that people could buy or get for free after watching something on C4, to learn more, get help or celebrate the subject. Someone had the bright idea of putting the content of the booklets online, well before the main Channel 4 website was created, and I learned on the job from then.

As this was back in 1997, there weren't many courses on the subject of web writing but over the last ten years Nancy has attended a range of courses. She says:

> I went to a good one-day 'user-centred design' course at the University of Westminster, run by New Media Knowledge (www.nmk.co.uk), a useful organization. I also took a course, Onscreen Editing 1 and 2, from the Society for Editors and Proofreaders (www.sfep.org.uk) which was good, very thorough; I picked up a lot of tips that have helped me edit other people's work more easily.

Nancy now co-tutors at the Publishing Training Centre in Wandsworth (www.train4publishing.co.uk) on their writing and editing for the web courses and runs occasional in-house courses.

Nancy's background was in book editing, which she still does occasionally alongside work for a range of clients. She says, 'Going back to editing books has been interesting – it shows how different they are from websites, which I now much prefer.'

Nancy is now the editor of the C4 History website, www.chan nel4.com/history. She says, 'Most of its content has been commissioned, edited or written by me. However, in January 2007, the budget for my work was cut by 90 per cent; now, I update the C4 History homepage and write the occasional bit of content, a thousand words here, a thousand words there.' Nancy is also the internet director of the Society for Editors and Proofreaders. To make up for the cut in work from C4, Nancy is working for a government department on their external website. She explains:

> I am revamping one large part of it and creating a general communications section on their intranet. This work has involved everything from information architecture and web design to editing and rewriting bits of content, plus being trained in how to input directly on to the department intranet. I really like the work and the people, but find the commuting difficult after many years of working from home.

Blogging

Do you have a blog? A blog, or weblog, is simply a regularly updated journal published on the internet. A personal blog can be a great place to write down odd ideas and short bits of inspiration that may or may not turn into something longer. It can act as a showcase for your work as a writer too: many journalists use blogs in this way. Media companies now produce blogs instead of or alongside print magazines, with readers checking out new content every day. And businesses may use blogs to bring customers their latest news. If you want to find out about what is going on in the world of blogs, Technorati (www.technorati.com) monitors millions of blogs and what it calls 'citizen media', independent, user-generated photos, videos, etc. You can get paid to blog, or set up your own income-generating blog: read on to find out more.

Blogs are simple to set up. You can use one of a range of providers of blog-ware, including:

- Typepad, www.typepad.com
- Blogger, www.blogger.com
- Wordpress, www.wordpress.com
- Movable Type, www.movabletype.org

Some sites offer hosting or you can host the site elsewhere. With many you can buy your own web address and point it to the site, so instead of having an address like www.yourname.wordpress.com, you could simply have www.yourname.com, which makes it easier to find the site, and hence will improve your number of visitors. Check the small print before choosing your blog host and software provider, as some have clauses that allow them to claim copyright on everything on their site.

Diane Shipley
Diane Shipley specializes in technology, books, entertainment and lifestyle journalism for print and web publications. She writes for publications including *Easy Living*, the *Telegraph*, *Essentials* and *Mslexia* and as the new technology expert for *Woman's Weekly*.

211

Diane has been writing since the end of an enforced break due to illness. She says:

> As I started to recover, an old ambition to be a journalist reasserted itself. I began by contributing occasional pieces to ME charity newsletters and magazines, and in October 2005 I set up a blog, www.dianeshipley.com, which gave me a showcase for my writing and a way to interact with other writers, which was fantastic after spending a long time housebound.

Diane started contributing unpaid reviews to a book blog, as well as pitching to other publications. She says:

> I got a couple of small commissions accepted and decided that I would only take on paid writing work, which meant no more reviews. Then around the end of June I got an email from the site, asking me if I'd like to write for them, paid. Within a couple of weeks, the existing editor left, and I was asked if I'd like to become joint editor of the site. This was really my big break: as I was blogging for a living, the *Telegraph* and *Mslexia* asked me to write about blogging for them. I pitched an idea to the *Guardian* blog, using the fact that I was editor of the site as leverage. That was one of the most controversial blogs they've ever had, and helped me make a name for myself! I've since written ten more pieces for them and that's been a great credit to have on my CV. In fact, when I recently pitched the editor of Handbag.com she recognized my name from the *Guardian* blog. I was also commissioned to write a first-person piece for the *Guardian* Education website last year, and used my *Guardian* blog pieces as writing samples. I also write about technology for popular US website Popgadget (www.popgadget.net) on a daily basis, which I love.

Making money from your own blog

You may be one of the lucky few whose personal blog gets found by a publisher, leading to a generous book deal. If you want to increase the chances of this, you probably also need to follow the traditional route of writing a synopsis and a few chapters and sending them to publishers and agents, as they are unlikely to simply stumble across your site. Perhaps more practically, you can also look at making money from your own blog: here are a few tips on how to do it. Post every day, and build an audience by posting comments on other people's sites and including links in your posts. Make sure that your blog is covering a focused niche: it is much harder to promote a blog that is just 'all about me' than one which covers a topic of interest. The benefit of the web is that, whatever your interest, it is possible to get in touch with others with the same fascination for the topic, who will avidly follow whatever you blog. List your site on blog directories like Technorati, www.technorati.com, and Bloglines, www.bloglines. com. You can then add features such as advertising, through GoogleAdSense and the many other advertising programmes that link the adverts displayed to your content, or set up a bookshop with books on relevant topics via Amazon Associates. There are other affiliate programmes where you make a small percentage of sales generated by clicks from your site too: see Clickbank, www.clickbank.com, and Commission Junction, www.cj.com. This is not going to cover all your bills, but if you are canny about using the right keywords and developing a good following for the blog it can provide a useful addition to your income. You might then go on to create an e-book to sell, create a course or offer consultancy in your specialist area to the followers of your blog, all of which will boost the chances of making a living income. Finally, you could pop a 'tip jar' on your blog and ask for donations from readers.

Patricia says:

This year I am focusing on writing books and blogging on issues affecting women over forty, at www.secondcherry.com. I aim to make the website profitable, and am also looking to gain a book contract from the blog. I usually blog in the mornings, then do my shopping, housework, exercise, etc. Then have lunch, prepare another blog in the afternoon and aim to write 1–2,000 words on my book.

Paid blogging

Media outlets like national newspapers the the *Guardian*, the *Telegraph* and *The Times* and the BBC have their own websites and pay bloggers to contribute on a regular basis. There are also blog networks like Shiny Media, Weblogs Inc and Gawker Media, which run a range of blogs and pay contributors per post. You can earn from a few pounds for a post on some sites, or be paid by the word, but usually at slightly lower rates than print journalism. Other sites may offer a percentage of ad revenue.

Keris Stainton

Keris Stainton was an accounts administrator in corporate recovery and personal insolvency when she started her blog in 2003. Inspired by chick lit author Jennifer Weiner's blog, Keris blogged every morning, taking her mind away from the job. She says, 'My work was not just boring, it was depressing too as I dealt with calls from people who were in panic and distress.' Keris was already writing fiction, and working with a life coach, Suzy Greaves, to help her finish a book and look for a publisher. She says, 'I told Suzy about how I hoped to get a book deal and leave work, but she asked me why I was waiting for the book deal. If I found work so depressing, what else could I do? She also pointed out that a book deal might only bring in a few thousand pounds.' Keris had left school wanting to be a journalist, but never got very far with this idea. This time, though, with Suzy's guidance, she started pitching. Keris explains, 'I had thought that I needed to go on a course or get journalism experience, but of course I had been writing fiction and blogging for some time, so I wasn't a novice writer.' Keris used her blogging experience as the basis of her first pitch. She says, 'I sent a pitch to *Essentials*, and it was the first idea they'd had on the subject of blogging. I was delighted when they commissioned me to write 1,200 words on the subject. I wrote the article to length, but told the editor I had additional material, and ended up being paid for an 1,800 word piece.' Keris has since had articles based on blogging in *Cosmo Girl*, *Mslexia*, and *A Place in the Sun – Essentially America*. She says, 'I am interested in writing about blogging. It lets me spend time finding interesting blogs and sharing them with other people.'

Keris stumbled across chick lit blog Trashionista.com, which is run by Shiny Media, and started submitting reviews. She says:

> I'd sent in about ten reviews when the editor left and I was asked if I'd like to share the role with another freelancer. I now edit Trashionista and write for several other Shiny Media blogs, Bag Lady, Bridalwave, Dollymix and TV Scoop. I do three posts a day for Trashionista, the Bag Lady and Bridalwave, plus a review for TV Scoop a couple of times a week. I love writing book reviews, but it can sometimes be harder to come up with ideas on weddings or bags. I get paid per post, which can mean I'm getting the same few pounds whether I write thirty words or a 1,200-word column. However, it is great to know that I have regular money coming in and it takes the pressure off when I'm pitching.

If you are setting up a personal blog, Keris advises, 'Don't worry about who is reading, just be honest and open. I've made lots of genuine friends through my blog. It takes trial and error to get a blog looking good: my first blog looked hideous. There are lots of online tutorials, and you don't need to know lots of html.'

Keris now has a book deal, and she feels her blog has helped achieve this. She says, 'When sending pitches and proposals, I've been able to point editors and agents to my website where they can get a much better idea about me and my writing style. I've uploaded book extracts too. The feedback from strangers has helped increase my confidence too.'

If you're trying to monetize a site, bear in mind that you need plenty of visitors. Keris says, 'I think you need to develop a niche too. I never made money from Google AdWords; now I simply have ads for products that I really like. I do know people with more business-based sites that are making £100 a month from ads, so it can work.'

Setting up your own website for profit

Many people start websites full of enthusiasm and ideas to turn the site into a paying business, but few succeed. Louisa Bird came up with the idea of the Women's Marketing Forum, a website for women business owners and entrepreneurs to link up with marketing experts, read their articles and get advice. Louisa explains:

> A lot of women love working for themselves but are uncomfortable with the marketing side. As well as my marketing training, I had also used my skills in practice promoting my e-commerce natural body products business in the early 90s, so I felt I had a lot to offer, and would get other experts on board to help too.

Louisa learnt a lot of the skills needed to set up and promote the site just by using the internet to find clients and promote her own business. The Women's Marketing Forum was initially a subscription service. Louisa says, 'This worked well up to a point. The subscription gave you access to forums and expert advice from me and other marketing specialists. However, some long-standing members didn't make the most of their subscription, and rarely or never asked for one-to-one e-coaching.'

Louisa has now relaunched the site. Membership is free, and users can post queries and get feedback on their marketing plans and materials. Louisa says:

> I think women are now used to getting free business support and funded training. At the moment the monetization of the site is purely through advertisements. As it develops and we get more members we will offer further services that members can opt to pay for, such as teleclasses. I want it to be more than just another social networking site. Users can learn how to get more clients, and read articles from me and guest bloggers all about marketing.

Another site that is working successfully is ilikemusic.com. The site has grown enormously since it was started in 2001, and editor

Cheryl Rickman explains how she has contributed to this growth:

> Initially it was my knowledge of who to contact in order to set up interviews and knowing how to write news stories and features and conduct interviews themselves. But my web skills also came in to play when deciding on the 'hierarchy of information', the order for the menu of content. Now I am mainly responsible for setting up and conducting interviews and rewriting punchy keyword-rich news items in my own words, as ilikemusic.com is a supplier of music news to Google News. I also act as a consultant when it comes to site revamps.

If you are planning your own website, Cheryl advises:

> Develop a site that is usable, easy to navigate, search-engine friendly and content-rich with fresh informative and useful content. You need a website that encourages return visits and, equally, you need a business that serves customers well enough to encourage repeat custom and referrals. Be open to learning, always. The web is a changing platform and those who think they know it all in business don't last long. Make sure your copy is clear, crisp and compelling and that the design of your website creates the right perception.

Other types of work

If you have marketing or/and copywriting skills, you may find your niche in various sorts of writing for the web. You could specialize in email marketing, writing sales letters and adverts for companies to send to their online databases. Businesses may need copywriters to create online advertisements for pay-per-click and other advertising. Creating an online ad that gets people to click through to the advertiser's site is a specific art. There are also opportunities to create content for companies wanting to use SMS or text messages to contact customers and advertise their services. The SMS messages can be the actual service, containing a regular snippet of information for the subscribers.

Joanne Mallon says:

I was contracted to write some inspirational text messages. I was limited to 120 characters, which suited my compact writing style. This was for a subscription service, and they wanted someone with a personal development background who could also write. It is great to build up a market for writing using your own background: you don't need fifty years of experience to be able to write or talk about it.

New media, new career?

So, are you ready to make a career out of online writing? Before you get started ask yourself:

- Do I have relevant experience and skills? If not, start writing some online features or create your own blog.
- What niche or specialism can I develop?
- What area of online writing do I want to make a living from?
- How am I going to make my online writing pay the bills?

Make an action plan to help you resolve any issues raised by these questions and you will soon be ready to start making a living writing for the web.

Chapter 11

Other writing-related work

There are many other careers where writing plays a large part, or where you are working with the written word in one way or another. Consider:

- coaching
- ghost-writing
- indexing
- proofreading
- speechwriting.

In this chapter there is brief advice about how to get started, plus details of professional organizations or training providers, where they exist, so you can find out more.

Coaching

Personality
If you love giving advice, you might think being a coach is for you. It is a lot more than just giving advice, though. Trained coaches are able to help their clients analyse and reflect on their

current situation and work on their future goals and plans. If you relate well to people, can listen patiently and provide helpful and thought-provoking insights to a situation, you might want to think of training as a coach. You need to be generous with ideas, support-ive, non-judgemental, and want to help people too.

Writing and coaching

Coaching is included in this section as it is a career that seems to appeal to many writers, especially journalists or those with a non-fiction specialism. Some coaches set up business specializing in coaching others to help them develop their writing skills, complete a novel or get a publishing deal. Coaching is a career than can run alongside a freelance writing career: if you have a specialism and experience this can be an advantage and help you attract clients looking to succeed in the same niche market.

Skills

If you want to become a coach, you will need a range of skills to help your clients develop their full potential. You should be able to help a client explore their needs, motivations and desires. You should be skilled at drawing out the client's own assets and assist-ing their thought processes. You should be used to using a range of questioning techniques to encourage your client to go further and work out their own solutions, set goals and break their aims down into achievable steps.

Knowledge

If you work as a coach you will need to have a range of techniques and tools at your fingertips. You will find it useful to have knowledge of one-to-one training, facilitating and counselling. A coaching course will teach you how to use tools like the GROW model, a way of structuring a coaching session. The session starts as you and your client identify their goal for the discussion, which will tie in with their long term-aim. Then you help the client look at the Reality, getting an accurate picture of the current situation. A coach will then move the client to look at his or her options, being careful to draw as many suggestions as possible from the client and adding some suggestions himself or herself where needed. The final part, the Wrap-up, is where the coach gets the client to commit to action and define a plan. In this stage you might also break the plan down into steps and work out a timescale to achieve them. As a coach you should be able to evaluate the outcomes for each client, based on objective measures set at the start of each series of coaching sessions.

Experience
If you aspire to become a coach, all sort of life experience will help, and may enable you to find a niche. You will probably be asked to go through some coaching yourself; that is the way many people decide that they want to be a coach.

Professional organizations and training providers
Middlesex University, the University of Leeds, Sheffield Hallam University and Oxford Brookes University all offer coaching training, and there is a large number of private training providers too. You can pick the mode of study that suits you. Many courses are designed for people who are moving from another career, so are offered part time, in evenings and over weekends, or by distance learning. Visit the Coaching and Mentoring Network's website, www.coachingnetwork.org.uk, for a list of course providers.

You might want to join an organization like the International Coach Federation, www.coachfederation.org, for access to conferences, events and ongoing training.

Getting work
You usually need to find individual clients for coaching. When you are training you will work with people on a free or low-cost basis, and some of these may turn into full paying clients. Tell everyone about your new career, and get some cards printed to hand out. You could leave cards in places like business centres or complementary therapy practices. Many people will search for a coach online, so a clear website setting out your services can be a good advertisement. Look at earlier chapters for more advice on putting the word out about your business.

Getting paid

Coaches' charges vary enormously. At the top end, big business coaches with high profiles can charge thousands of pounds for a few sessions. When starting up, you may offer sessions for a much lower fee. Canny coaches work out subscription plans, giving discounts for clients who sign up and pay for a number of sessions in advance. It really comes down to pitching a price and seeing how much work you generate, which in turn may depend on how good you are at promoting your services. In time you can establish a fee level that enables you to cover your living and business costs for a reasonable number of hours' work.

Joanne Mallon

Joanne Mallon offers life and career coaching for media professionals. She coaches aspiring writers and journalists, TV producers and presenters as well as those who have a media career which they want to develop. Joanne offers media training for business too, through face-to-face workshops and teleclasses. She combines coaching with continuing her own media work. She is regularly interviewed on radio and TV, and writes for newspapers and magazines, her own and other blogs. She has published an e-book, *The Beginner's Guide to TV Interviews*, which is available from her site www.medialifecoach.com.

Joanne spent the first five years of her working life as a civil servant, saying, 'My dad working in the Civil Service, and coming from working-class Belfast, I felt I might as well have dreamt of being a spaceman as becoming a journalist.' Despite this, Joanne had an early passion for the media, and was involved in a weekly slot on a youth programme on local radio. She then took the plunge at the age of twenty-two and went to university, where she studied English and communication and wrote regularly for the university newspaper. She followed her degree with a post-graduate Diploma in Broadcast Journalism at Cardiff, which led to a career working on programmes including *GMTV*, *Vanessa* and *This Morning*. Joanne decided that she wouldn't work in TV for ever, and took a diploma course through the Coaching Academy. This involved a residential weekend and home study. Joanne comments, 'I had to write essays, and get lots of practical experience. You could do the course at your own pace: I took four months but some people took up to two years. I felt that I wanted to know more, and then went on to do the neurolinguistic programming practitioner training.' Joanne opted for a course that involved four days' training once a month over a period of four months.

If you are thinking of becoming a coach, Joanne advises:

> There are no national minimum standards for coaching at the moment. Choose your course carefully, as some courses have excellent marketing, but aren't as good in reality. Ask a number of coaches where they trained. Find out what they thought about the course. Think about whether you learn best in a short but intense course, or with work spread out over a longer period. Would you prefer face-to-face teaching, home learning or teleclasses? If you want to become a corporate coach, there are courses that focus on that. However, in reality, clients don't choose you for the letters after your name. They want to feel confidence in you.

She says, 'As a coach you touch on so many different aspects of people's lives there is always a need to know more. I still do various short courses in subjects such as time management.'

Ghost-writing

A ghost-writer is paid to write books, articles or even blogs which are credited to another person.

Personality
If you want to be a ghost-writer, you may be someone who is content to stay out of the limelight, or you might enjoy a close brush with someone famous, without having all the downsides of fame yourself. You need to be able to listen to someone else's concerns: the subject of the book you are writing may be trusting you with personal information.

Writing style

As a ghost-writer, the most important element of writing style is the ability to assess and replicate someone else's style. You need to be able to keep to their style consistently too. You may want to focus on writing full-length books, the perhaps more traditional perception of a ghost-writer, or write articles and features on behalf of someone else. Business owners may be keen to raise their profile as an expert, yet lack the writing skills necessary. You need to be able to read their target publication, assess its preferred style and combine that with something that sounds as if it genuinely comes from the person commissioning you to write.

Skills

You need to be good at collaboration. From before you even start writing it can be helpful to spend some time evaluating each party's motivation for taking part in the project. Having goals in common can help keep the project on track. You should have experience of interviewing people and be able to demonstrate your writing skills.

Knowledge

As an aspiring ghost-writer you need to have all the skills of a good journalist (see Chapter 9). You will impress clients, publishers and agents with flawless grammar and spelling, or lose their interest rapidly if you don't have the skills they are after. Beyond journalistic skills, if you have to write someone's life story you need to be able to pull out the salient facts and structure information so that over the course of 50,000 or 100,000 words you can capture and keep the reader's interest. If you want to find out more, *Ghostwriting* is one of the best books on the subject, written by the prolific ghost-writer Andrew Crofts.

Experience

You may not be able to start with a big celeb: if you know someone with a fascinating story, you may want to talk to them about writing their story, create an agreement between the two of you and then start looking for a publisher. Alternatively, do you know someone who is an expert who might be interested in raising their own profile by collaborating in a book? You get the benefit of their expertise and they benefit from your writing skills.

Getting work

The key aspect to generating work is letting people know you are available. Tell everyone you know about your ghost-writing service. If you have media contacts, that's great, but one of your friends or relatives may also know someone useful. People who are looking for a ghost-writer may search online, so set up a simple website promoting your services. You can also go through a directory such as the *Writers' and Artists' Yearbook* to contact publishers and agents, but you may need to write hundreds of letters to generate a response. Include the compelling benefits of working with you in your letter, and highlight specialist experience that the publisher won't be able to find elsewhere.

You may need to persuade your subject that you are the best person to write about them, which is where examples of your work are invaluable. You may need to have written a number of books yourself before being sought out to get involved with a ghost-writing project. Publishers will be looking for writers with a solid track history to handle celebrity biographies. While you may think of ghost-writers who create books for celebs and politicians, there is a growing market for ghosted blogs, where you post regularly to a blog on behalf of a business or individual.

Getting paid

As a ghost-writer you may find clients pay you themselves, or you may work up a sample chapter on spec and send it to a publisher in the hope of getting an advance and royalties. If working directly with clients you could ask to be paid per word or offer a flat fee, depending on the nature of the project, the length of the work and the complexity of the research you are required to do. It helps if you have a rough idea of how many words you can write per month, or how many months you would need to write a certain length of book. Consider how you will split any post-publishing royalties. Before agreeing to any ghost-writing, you should take advice on a contract. And don't forget to decide about expenses in advance: who will pay for train or plane tickets and hotel bills if you are required to travel while researching the book?

Professional organizations

The Society of Authors offers a free contract advice service to members and has published a booklet on ghost-writing and collaborative agreements. It advises you to agree details such as when and how often you will meet, the sort of materials you, the writer, will have access to, and whether copyright is owned jointly. You should establish whether you will receive a credit on the cover, a mention within the book or be asked to sign an agreement not to reveal your involvement at all.

Cheryl Rickman
Cheryl Rickman's first ghost-written book was published in 2007. She got into ghost-writing after writing *The Small Business Start-Up Workbook* (www.smallbusinessworkbook.com). Cheryl was interviewing Peter Jones for *Better Business* magazine, when he mentioned he was struggling to make progress writing his own book. Cheryl explains how she saw an opportunity in what he said:

> I mentioned that I'd written my own book, which was selling well and had a Foreword by Dame Anita Roddick and that I was also a web copywriting expert. Subsequently, he invited me to his office and gave me a test project to see if I could write in his voice, writing copy for his website. I completed this and then kept emailing him suggesting I might help him with his own book. I had no idea of how to price this or the procedures involved, but came up with a quote that was reasonable and he persuaded his publishers that he'd like to use me for the book, rather than using one of their own writers. The deadline was approaching as he had a TV series that the book tied in with, so I was given the project and completed the book, with lots of input from Peter, within three months.

The book has since become a *Sunday Times* bestseller and Cheryl has impressed the publishers enough for them to consider her for future ghost-writing projects. She has a few tips for anyone who would like to start ghost-writing:

> I was very fortunate and made the most of opportunities presented to me. I've managed to do all of this without any representation from an author's agent or similar. And, by doing a good job for Peter and impressing the publishers (one of the top five publishers in the UK), I've done more work for Peter and will be considered for other ghost-writing projects by the publishers. It gave me an inroad that many writers take years to achieve. Ensure you've written at least one book of your own before approaching those you'd love to ghost-write a book for. When it comes to writing, it's vital to write in the voice of the 'author' so you need to get to know the person you are writing for and, ideally, see some of their own written work (it may be a portion of a diary, or they may have started writing their own book). Seize opportunities and network to gain contacts. Writing is only half the battle; you need to be good at communicating so you can liaise effectively with the publishers and the 'author' during the writing process.

Indexing

The work
Indexers work with books and other documents, devise index terms, and create and organize an index.

Personality
If you are interested in indexing, you need to be a stickler for accuracy. Indexers need to be able to work concisely and precisely, and cope with an intellectually demanding task over a sustained period. Alongside these task-related traits, you also need to be flexible and adaptable: you may be called upon to meet tight deadlines or work antisocial hours. You also need good negotiation skills to ensure that you run a profitable business.

Knowledge

Most indexers have degree-level qualifications. If you have an area of specialist subject knowledge this can be an advantage and provide you with a niche. You'll need to keep your specialist knowledge up to date.

Professional organizations and training providers

The main professional organization for Britain and Ireland is the Society of Indexers. The Society offers training, workshops, conferences and continuing professional development as well as information for publishers on commissioning indexes and an online directory of qualified indexers. The Society of Indexers awards its own qualifications. You can study to become an indexer through its distance learning course, which has four units with tests at the end of each. The course is around fifty hours' work and can be taken over one to a maximum of five years. There are optional workshops to help you develop your skills. You then are required to index a book or document of your choice. If you complete the course successfully you become an Accredited Indexer, and are entitled to a listing in the Society directory. If you get more experience you can then go on to apply for Fellowship.

Who might require the work?

Indexes are mainly required by publishers, especially those specializing in academic and business books.

Getting work

Once you have trained, an entry in the Society of Indexer's directory, *Indexers Available*, is a good start to finding work. Your areas of specialist knowledge can also be key, so take some time to find out about publishers that cover this area. As with many areas covered in this book, persistence is also important. When starting up, you will need to make contact with what seems like an enormous number of publishers before striking lucky. The Society of Indexers advises that its local groups and email group can be good sources of information on work opportunities.

Getting paid

Indexers may charge by the hour or by the page, or negotiate a fixed fee for a job. The more experience you have, the more you can charge, and more complex and highly specialized work commands higher rates. You may also put your rates up for work to a tight deadline.

Many indexers combine indexing with activities such as copy-editing and proofreading, which gives you a bit of variety and can help even out the flow of work.

Ann Hall

Ann Hall had been working as a teacher, but gave up this career when she had her first child. This was when she first thought of becoming an indexer. She explains how it happened.

> I was stuck at home with my first child and he had reached the grand old age of one year. I was beginning to go ever so slightly bonkers and wished I was back teaching. Then I heard a programme on the radio, which extolled the virtues of indexing – all you needed were some file cards and a box to put them in and a few reference books.

When Ann was looking into changing careers there was a dearth of courses on indexing. She says, 'I taught myself by reading everything I could find on the subject. I then did research in Leeds Public Library non-fiction department, choosing a large number of books at random and studying the indexes in detail.' Ann then launched herself into indexing, which was, she says, 'The best decision I ever made. It changed my life in many ways and I'm still addicted to it – aforementioned first-born is now thirty-nine. My kids grew up thinking that indexing was what mums did and couldn't believe that their friends at school had mums who made beds and vacuumed all day.'

Ann joined the Society of Indexers, and promoted her services through an entry in their booklet *Indexers Available*. After a few years of indexing and successful completion of 'Registration', where an index is assessed by experienced indexers, she offered to help assess others. She says, 'I thus became known in the Society as someone interested in teaching others (once I had found out what a satisfying job indexing was, I was full of proselytizing zeal).' In 1983, Michael Gordon, the founder of indexing course Book Indexing Postal Tutorials, asked Ann to take over his training programme. Ann now runs the renamed email indexing course, Book Indexing Personal Tutorials.

If you want to get into indexing, Ann has some advice based on almost forty years in the business:

> You need to be the sort of person who makes lists and enjoys sorting things into categories. A meticulous attention to detail is necessary as well as an ability to get into the minds of the potential users of the index. Just because you have chosen a main entry which you think is logical, it doesn't mean that the user of the index is going to think in the same way. So you have to provide a cross-reference to send the reader to the right place in the index. It's no good lumping together all the references to transport, for instance, into one big entry, with sub-entries for the main types of transport (for instance air, canals, rail, roads, etc.) unless you tell the index-user what you've done, with the use of cross-references. In this case, you would have 'air travel *see under* transport.'

> But you need to be flexible. At the end of the book you may decide that the transport entry has become far too unwieldy and then you may decide to reverse the process to make things easier for the reader. For example, you would create what I call a 'general reference entry' like the following: 'transport *see* air; canal; rail; road'.

Proofreading

A proofreader goes through copy before it goes to print, pulling out errors in spelling and grammar.

The work
A proofreader needs to check for:

- errors during typesetting;
- spelling mistakes;
- faulty punctuation and grammar errors;
- incorrect capitalization;
- inconsistencies with page numbers, headings, spellings, etc., (for example, if a character is referred to as Jon Smith on page 3, but John Smith at all other times, this needs to be rectified);
- layout problems, such as changes in font;
- conformity to reference systems and the client's house style (for example, dates, abbreviations and numbers can be written out differently depending on the client's preference);
- amendments made by the copy-editor.

Personality
Like indexers, anyone entering into proofreading needs to have an excellent attention to detail. You need to be able to concentrate on the fine details, rather than being someone who looks only at the bigger picture.

Skills and knowledge
A proofreader needs an excellent grasp of grammar and spelling. By the time you receive a text, if working for a big publisher, it will have been copy-edited. Small businesses may simply employ a proofreader, in which case you will also need to be able to spot inconsistencies in the text. You may need to check page numbering and details such as whether diagrams and illustrations are numbered and referred to correctly. Also, it may be necessary to check one version of the document against another. You will need to know the set of symbols used in book production by copy-editors and proofreaders.

Rach Colling offers proofreading for websites. She says:

> If I'm editing or writing new stuff for a website, sometimes I'll have access to a client's content management system, so I can make the amendments direct. Other times it can be a case of emailing them a word document with new text, or a report of the proofreading

errors. Several times for proofreading and editing, the client's requested I print out the pages from the website, and send them back with everything marked on in red pen, which is very satisfying.

Professional organizations and training providers

Join the Society for Editors and Proofreaders, which offers a range of training courses, conferences and a magazine. Its website, www.sfep.org.uk, has plenty of advice for anyone thinking of going into proofreading.

Who might require the work?

You may decide to specialize in proofing books, websites, magazines or other publicity materials and publications. As with many of the areas discussed in this book, specialist knowledge can be an advantage. The Society for Editors and Proofreaders advises that, in a competitive area like proofreading:

> If you have expertise in a particular subject, you may stand a better chance of finding work with publishers producing publications in your subject. For example, if you have a degree in engineering or law, or can cope with complex mathematics, you will probably get more business coming your way than if you are hoping to work on the latest bestselling novels.

Getting work

Once you have decided on a niche, list all the businesses that might need work. If you want to work in a certain sort of publishing, use directories like the *Writers' and Artists' Yearbook*, and start calling round relevant organizations to find named individuals who might commission proofreaders. Then write in with details of your service and experience. If you have some contacts this can help speed up the process: otherwise you may find you have to send a lot of letters before generating work. You may find it easier to broaden your approach, and look at all the different businesses that might produce any print materials. Small and medium enterprises may be keen to find someone to check their website;

companies may need a proofreader for their annual report. Again, make a list of businesses to contact, find the name of the person who handles their publications and get in touch by phone to tell them about your services. Follow up by sending a copy of your flyer or CV.

The SfEP produces a *Directory of Editorial Services* where you can promote your proofreading business. The organization suggests joining with other complementary freelances, such as designers, typesetters and translators, to advertise a one-stop shop. Proofreader Ruth Rayment says, 'For obtaining work, I recommend getting a website, and joining directories. Proofreaders are needed by lots of different people, not just publishing houses these days. Most of my work has been for companies who provide reports to their clients, and I have also done work for a few students.'

Getting paid

Proofreading isn't the highest paid profession. The SfEP suggests, at time of writing, charging a minimum rate of around £19.25 an hour. It offers a 'Rate for the Job' page on its website, where members can see what others have charged.

Ruth Rayment

Ruth Rayment was an admin manager for a small company, but now offers proofreading for businesses through her website, www.r2proofreading.co.uk. She explains how she got started:

> The idea came to me while I was driving to work one morning, worrying about whether my job was safe. I had a small child and was hoping to have another baby, and my part-time hours fitted my life with my daughter perfectly. I was worried that, if I had to change jobs, I wouldn't find something else as flexible. Proofreading seemed to be a field that was in demand as I was always spotting errors in printed material. I took advice from my husband, family and friends and they have all been incredibly supportive. The outlay is quite small, with very few expenses, no staff to employ and therefore not too much admin to complete. As it happened, I then had another baby and used my time on mater-

nity leave to really investigate the business start-up procedure and complete my course.

Ruth took a home study course. She says:

> A close friend had also done a home study course which she lent to me. This meant that I had two courses to study. There were no time restraints, so I took it slowly, doing lots of extra reading and practice. I did feel that the course seemed a bit old-fashioned, focusing mainly on working with hard copies and publishing houses, and not touching much on using computers for editing. So far, I have done a bit of proofreading on paper, but not for publishing houses, so the symbols I learnt during my studies don't mean much to my clients. My course also focused on setting up a business, including tips on how to invoice clients and keep records, which was very helpful.

Ruth's first step in business was to set up her own website. She says:

> I researched it quite a bit, to find the right provider and to see what my competition were up to, and had quite a firm idea of what I wanted the site to look like and how I wanted to sell my services. I have quite a silly sense of humour and didn't want to come across as a schoolmarm, instead wanting to be seen as an approachable person. I have learnt a lot about search-engine optimization and free marketing and feel that the website is the best thing I could have done as it is working for me twenty-four hours a day.

Ruth looked at a range of ways of promoting her services as a proofreader. She says:

> The scary thing is cold calling. I decided not to contact publishing houses initially, but to focus on small businesses in the digital and print media. I created a list from the local *Yellow Pages* and starting phoning around. I had a lot of people saying 'No' but also a lot of positive feedback. I decided to try and do a few minutes a day and to try to end on a positive comment, to make me want to get on the

phone again the next day. The irony is that most of my clients have found me and not the other way round. Networking is also a scary thing, but I have found that the more people you talk to, the more likely they are to say, 'My husband's a printer; give me your details,' or something similar. I haven't gone to any networking events yet, but did make a useful contact through Ecademy and she put a client in touch with me. I'm quite happy to help other people if I can, as I seem to have picked up a lot of information over the first year. I have signed up to a lot of newsletters for small businesses: www.freelanceuk.com offers practical advice to people working from home. I have found Business Link to be a wonderful resource, especially their free workshops. One speaker in particular, whose training course I attended before starting up, was so inspiring that I came away determined to make a go of it and put all her tips into practice.

Now Ruth has been in business for a year, she has a good idea of the skills she uses most as a proofreader. She says:

Attention to detail is the main skill. I hadn't realized quite how pedantic I was about not just spelling, grammar and punctuation, but also about headings being consistent and tab indentations lining up. I always read a text at least twice to make sure I haven't missed anything. I keep lists of words I have looked up so that I can refer back to them and notes on how my clients like to do things. I also find my four 'bibles' are invaluable: *Hart's Rules*, *New Oxford Spelling Dictionary*, *New Oxford Dictionary for Writers and Editors* and AskOxford (the online version of the *Oxford English Dictionary*).

Speechwriting

Personality
If you want to be a speechwriter, you need to be able to understand what makes people tick. As well as being good with words, the ability to put yourself in the place of your speaker and understand what will appeal to his or her audience is essential.

Writing style and skills

Writing for speeches can be very different from writing for any print media. You need to be able to write as people speak. As with ghost-writing, you need to be able to take on board your client's voice and style too. You need to be able to liaise with clients, handle their feedback and create a speech that will really ring true when they deliver it.

Knowledge

As a speechwriter you need to be able to research and become an expert in any topic you are writing on. For many jobs, though, you will be able to use the client's materials and expertise as your basis. Developing a niche or specialism can help you find and retain clients. A handy file full of quotes for every occasion is a useful thing for every speechwriter to acquire. Keep a file of jokes, quotes and interesting snippets so you always have something to illustrate a point or make people laugh in a speech. The internet makes it much easier to find this sort of information nowadays, but keeping your own file can give you access to things you won't find online.

Caroline Lashley
Caroline Lashley runs Bulletpoint PR Training. She has advice for anyone wanting to start writing speeches professionally:

> These days, the trend for a good speech has moved away from boring, long-winded sermons to seconds-long, sexy and memorable sound-bites. A good speech lies somewhere in the middle. If you're writing a speech it can be an exercise fraught with linguistic mine-fields, so here are some guidelines to help you be successful.
>
> Write for the ear: it sounds obvious, but if you write for print media it can be easy to forget that speechwriting is essentially writing to be heard. If you're not used to writing for the ear, listen to the radio or to television news reporters. If you're more of an online person, then listening to factual or speech-based podcasts is a useful way to go to get a sense of what works for the ear. Often speeches – especially made famous like the Martin Luther King's 'I

have a dream' and 'From the mountaintop' speeches – have a musical, rhythmical quality to them. Yes, MLK was a preacher and orator, but a good speech should contain a 'song' to keep listeners interested and, more importantly, listen and hear more clearly your message.

Plan: like presentations, speeches need to be planned. It's a bit like that oft-quoted piece of advice, 'fail to plan, then plan to fail'. For a speaker, failing in front of a live audience is a top nightmare, and if that happens, guess who gets the blame? Yep, the speech-writer: it's your job to make the speaker sound good. Get to know your speaker's aims and objectives, book time with your speaker and include him/her in the plan (it's in their interest, after all) and get an idea of what they're about and the audience that they are going to meet.

Interview your speaker and record your interview. You'll need to listen to their speech pattern, the tone, the pitch, their voice and how they use it, listen to the vocabulary and syntax construction used. All this information is vital, because when it comes to writing that speech, you'll have a good idea and sense of what your speaker is like. Don't forget, you are dealing with egos and credibility, yours and theirs.

Choose a good topic: this task may fall to you but let the speaker have some input: the speech has to sound as though he or she has written it. After all, the speaker is the one facing the audience, not you. Make sure it's a topic which allows you to showcase your talents as a speechwriter and displays your speaker's enthusiasm and passion.

Write your speech: give yourself a deadline (besides the official one) to write a draft version for your speaker to review, then you have time to make amendments if it's not hitting the spot. Write for the ear, and get as close as you can to your speaker's personal style, aims and objectives. Bear in mind the occasion you are writing for. Make that speech riveting for the audience: this is probably the hardest part to get right and this is where knowledge of the likely audience is important. Get your speaker to time and pace that speech: for most speakers, the optimum time is about twenty minutes: often, it's less.

When it's all over: if it went well, don't forget to pitch yourself for the next assignment. If it went less well, don't take it personally. Try to pinpoint where it didn't succeed so you can improve things for next time.

Experience
You should have some experience of public speaking, even if you prefer writing to standing up and delivering your work. Experience of speaking yourself is invaluable when it comes to knowing what will work well in front of an audience.

Professional organizations and training providers
There are plenty of companies set up to help you improve your speechwriting and presentation skills. Many of these are more aimed at business people who have to give presentations as part of their job. Check out the course content and make sure the information is pitched at the right level for someone who wants to become a professional speechwriter. There is no single organization for speechwriters: depending on your focus you might want to join Communicators in Business (see Chapter 5) or you may find membership of the Chartered Institute of Public Relations is useful (see Chapter 8).

Who might require the work?
People need speeches for a range of occasions. You may want to specialize in business, sales or promotional talks, or focus more on special occasions: a wedding is the time that many inexperienced speakers start looking for professional help. Many speechwriters, however, can turn their hand to any type of talk, given the right materials and time to research.

Getting work
A website is a useful advertisement, and can help people looking for a speechwriter to find you. If you want work with businesses, start to network, both online through sites like Ecademy, and face to face at your local business network or chamber of commerce. Alternatively, if you want to get work writing social speeches,

look at the hundreds of wedding sites and etiquette guides and get listed in their directories.

Terry

Terry is a speechwriter, and has been writing freelance for around twenty-five years. Before going freelance, Terry worked in financial services in marketing and events. He says:

> As part of the events we ran, we had to provide scripts for road shows which were mainly hosted by celebs. One year I really didn't like what the agency copywriter had come up with, so had a go myself. The client preferred my version too, and after that I wrote speeches and scripts for two or three road shows and product launches each year. I wrote for people like Angela Rippon, Noel Edmonds, Paul Daniels and Mike Yarwood.

Terry was made redundant from his job in financial services marketing after the financial markets crashed in 1987. He spent a brief while in another job, but swiftly decided he would rather work for himself and went freelance. One of his agency clients was very encouraging, offering to put work Terry's way, but, as Terry explains, the reality was different, 'Be cautious about people who encourage you to go freelance and offer freelance work. This man said he had a couple of big projects for me, but nothing ever materialized.'

Terry found starting out in freelance work very much feast or famine, both in terms of work and, as a result, income. He says:

> I'd get a big cheque for a job, spend all my time working on that and then get to the end and need to take time to find the next piece of work. It is hard as you almost need to be finding clients at the same time as you are working on your current project. It is also all too easy to take an afternoon off, then find you have to work to catch up. Many times I've found myself working late into the night to meet a deadline. You also have to do everything when you are your own boss, from doing the work to chasing payments to finding clients. I like writing, and found I often tended to leave the invoicing until I had to do it.

Terry offered a range of writing and marketing services and continued to write annual sales conference speeches and product launch scripts for contacts from past jobs. He says, 'A lot of the speechwriting work tends to be one-off, though, as people may ask you to write a speech for a special event.'

Terry has some tips for anyone thinking of speechwriting as a career. He says:

> I've read books on speechwriting, and some are better than others. It is easy to overanalyse it. I have run training and public speaking courses too. It is often a help to have experience of speaking yourself if you want to be a speechwriter: even if you are a bad public speaker it will give you a better understanding of what makes a good speech. Don't make it too short or too long. Make it precise, sharp and to the point. Get the audience's interest early. Think about what you're saying, who you are saying it to, and why you are saying it. Remember that someone will be saying what you write out loud. When writing speeches for other people you need to be aware of their style, personality and confidence. Some people aren't happy being funny, while others only want to be funny.

More ideas

If none of these ideas appeal you could also look into:

- policy research
- writing business plans
- creating puzzles and crosswords
- fundraising
- grant-writing
- writing for greetings cards.

Emily Adenipekun
Emily Adenipekun has been writing for four years, and has recently been working writing greeting cards on a freelance basis,

alongside her work running communication seminars and providing copywriting and effective language services to companies. She says, 'I love creating wording that will touch the person; make them laugh or bring a tear to their eyes.'

Emily got started by researching greeting card companies in the *Writers' and Artists' Yearbook*. She says, 'They have a list of greetings card companies. I call them up directly rather than send the words in "cold", and offer my services as a writer. They ask for some samples and will come back with a response in a week or two. If they like what they see, work will be offered.'

If you want to write greeting cards, Emily advises that you need the following skills:

- loving, appreciating, and being creative with, words;
- having the tenacity to get out there and do research, starting with reading the cards one gets from friends, family and acquaintances, and asking, 'Do they touch me? If yes, why? If not, why?' Then using the sentiment to work for you!
- being persistent; knowing one will get rejection, as well as commissions; asking for feedback.

As with any writing, you need to know your market and target your writing to your audience. Emily says, 'You must have an idea to whom you are communicating through these words on a well-decorated piece of card. Your message could change someone's life for the better.'

Conclusion

Whichever area appeals to you, here are a few final reminders on how to succeed:

- Brush up your skills.
- Choose a specialist area which makes the most of your expertise.
- Plan how you will promote your business.

- Tell everyone what you do, and the sort of work you are looking for.
- Network to find new contacts.
- Have a good website to showcase your portfolio.
- Offer excellent service and accurate work.
- Meet your deadlines.

Above all, remember that you will need to persist. It may take a year or even three to create a business that will earn you a living wage and keep you occupied full time. Alternatively, you may find the right niche first time and get your business paying the bills much sooner.

There will be times when you wonder whether you should find a more secure yet less interesting job. Stick with it, and find other people in a similar situation for support. Join a professional group, go to meetings and events, or even take time out to go for a walk with the dog or have a chat with someone to put everything in perspective. All small businesses go through ups and downs, and if you are working alone someone else's view can be invaluable.

Overall, though, I hope that you find lots of really interesting work and find that writing for a living is the right choice for you.

Appendix – Basics of grammar

Grammar is a set of rules to ensure that people can have a common understanding of the meaning of written text. If you want to earn your living from commercial writing, you need to have a good comprehension of the rules of grammar. Whether you are writing for a business client or producing copy for the local newspaper, your reputation will be damaged if the work you deliver is full of errors. Although writing for online purposes may sometimes be more informal, it is still essential to know and understand the rules of grammar, even if you choose to use a more relaxed style to suit the audience.

You may never have learnt grammar formally: most English speakers acquire their knowledge just from using the language. I learnt more about the structure of a language in French lessons that I was ever taught in English.

Here are a few essentials to remind you about the basics of grammar.

Common noun: the name of an object, place, person, animal or concept, like car, sheep, vase, house, etc.
book

Proper noun: a person or place name, starts with a capital. London, Mary, Monday. A book or film title is also a proper noun.
Alison

243

Pronoun: a word used in place of a noun. Personal pronouns include I, me, you, he, she, it. Possessive pronouns include mine, ours, his, hers, theirs. Reflexive pronouns include myself, himself. There are also demonstrative pronouns, like these or those, interrogative pronouns like who or what, relative pronouns like who and which, indefinite pronouns like everyone, someone, all or many.

She writes a book instead of *Mary writes a book.*

Think about how you use he/she. Some publications, such as women's magazines, will prefer to consistently use 'she'. Find out whether, when the gender of the subject is unknown, you should use the grammatically correct 'he or she' or the more easily read 'they'.

Adjective: a word to describe a noun, often ending in –ing, –y, –less, –ful, like blue, fast, small, interesting, windy, thoughtless, painful.

*She writes an **interesting** book.*

Verb: a 'doing' or 'being' word, which comes in different forms, like 'to write', writes, wrote or writing.

*She **writes.***

Adverb: a word to describe a verb. Close relations of adjectives, often ending –ly, like rapidly or interestingly, as well as words like well, always, otherwise.

*She writes **rapidly.***

Preposition: a word that goes before a noun, relating it to a verb, like in, through, on, at, with, in, as, by, to, from.

*She writes **in** a notebook.*

Conjunction: a joining word, like and, or, but, when, since, as.

*She writes at home **and** at work.*

Determiner: a word that comes before a noun (or noun phrase). 'The' is the definite article, and 'a' is known as an indefinite article. Other determiners include which, my, that.

*She is writing **a** book.*

244

Sentence structure

A sentence must almost always include a verb. Short exclamations are obvious exceptions to this rule.

A sentence is made up of words which can be grouped into phrases or clauses. A phrase is a group of words that work together, but cannot make sense alone outside the sentence.

*John writes **unpublishable drivel**.*

A clause is a group of words with a subject and related verb.

John is writing a book, while his housework remains ignored.

Think carefully about how you use clauses. A sentence usually includes one idea: this idea can be helpful when trying to ensure that your writing is clear. If your sentence contains several ideas, clauses and multiple phrases, try breaking it up or your meaning may be unclear.

Punctuation

Punctuation is there to help your readers understand what you have written. It can also help explain the feeling behind what you have written. There is a move to less punctuation: as an example, it is often acceptable to write 'etc' in the middle of a sentence without the traditional stop after to indicate the abbreviation. For clear writing style aim for commas only where needed.

Full stop: goes at the end of a sentence, when you have written a complete idea.

Comma: a comma has many functions to help a sentence make sense. It can indicate a different thought within a sentence.

John's book, once thought unpublishable, is now a best seller.

A comma can also set apart a name or names.

Ladies and gentlemen, we are pleased to present the first reading of John Jones's new best seller.

A comma should be used before a quote.

John said, 'I'm delighted with the sales of my book.'

Semi colon: this mark can split two parts of a single longer sentence, providing a more substantial pause than a comma.

Rebecca's celebrity interview proved popular; it increased the readership of that issue.

It has a useful function defining lists.

Rebecca's previous articles include Fake Tan Facts; Make-up Mysteries; Blusher Bloomer; and a series of readers' questions columns.

Colon: a colon can introduce a list, or lead to a conclusion, explanation or example. It is used when the second part of a sentence leads on from, yet is still strongly part of, the first.

It was obvious why Alison achieved career success: she was hardworking, never missed a deadline and her writing was outstanding.

It can also be used before a subtitle.

Alison Brown: My Writing Life

Brackets: part of a sentence can be set aside by putting it into brackets. You could do something similar with a pair of commas, depending on how much emphasis you want to give to each part of the sentence.

Tom Smith, formerly of Vogue, *is now writing for* Cosmopolitan.

Tom Smith (formerly of Vogue) *is now writing for* Cosmopolitan.

Within brackets, you can include additional information, an explanation, afterthought or clarification comment, aside or explanation.

Tom Smith is a talented young fashion writer (his specialism is women's catwalk trends).

Consider whether what you are writing would be clearer without brackets, and put the second idea into a separate sentence.

Tom Smith is a talented young fashion writer. His specialism is women's catwalk trends.

Dash: a dash is something that can interrupt a sentence, sharing this function with a colon. Possibly overused, it is seen more often in informal writing than in newspapers. As a hyphen, a dash is essential in the middle of some words.

Apostrophe: an apostrophe can be used to indicate a contraction, where two words have run together.
He can't get round to writing his second novel.
It can also indicate ownership:
Tom's book.
Watch out for pitfalls. Think about where to put the apostrophe after a plural noun. A book belonging to my parents is:
My parents' book.
'The writer's work' indicates the work of a single writer, whereas *'the writers' work'* would lead the reader to understand that the phrase referred to the work of several people. Without an apostrophe, *'the writers work'* has a different meaning again, work becoming a verb instead of a noun.

Pronouns such as his, hers and its do not take an apostrophe. 'It's' is a contraction of 'it is'.

Exclamation mark: this punctuation mark should not be overused, especially in business writing. Keep it for spoken phrases such as, *'Shut up!'* Do not use it to indicate you have said something funny: if the sentence is amusing the reader should be able to work it out without the exclamation mark.

Quotation marks: these are used to enclose words exactly as spoken, but not reported speech.
Mary said, 'I'm giving up writing novels: commercial copywriting is far more lucrative.'
Mary said that she was giving up writing novels as she had found commercial copywriting far more lucrative.
One debate may be about whether to use single or double quotes. As a business writer you should check whether the company or publication you are writing for has a house style.
Think carefully about how you punctuate the sentence within quotes: usually the punctuation mark goes inside the quotation marks:
John said, 'I'm amazed!'
If, however, the punctuation mark relates to the whole sentence it goes outside the quotation marks:

Was it tactless to say, 'My sales have beaten yours hands down'?

Bullet points: an essential for the modern writer, bullet points help you break down a list into one that can be seen more easily at a glance. Introduce a set of bullets with a colon.

A short bulleted list needs no punctuation bar a final full stop:

· *paper*

· *ink.*

A list using longer phrases can be punctuated with semi colons:

· *a good knowledge of grammar;*

· *the ability to spell;*

· *being widely read is an advantage.*

Finally, a list of complete sentences:

· *Then, you start each bullet with a capital and finish with a full stop.*

· *The next sentence follows the same format.*

Capitals and headlines: it is important to know when to capitalize a word: a dictionary is an essential guide if you are unclear. Even the most experienced writer may not remember that a Labrador takes a capital while a lurcher doesn't. When writing headlines, capitalize nouns and verbs, plus words of four letters of more. Short words like in, an, on and the will only take capitals if they start the headline.

However sure you are of your grammar, it is good to have your own guide to help you check your text. There are books that can help. Look at:

Essential English for Journalists, Editors and Writers, Harold Evans

Copyediting: A Practical Guide, Karen Judd.

If you want to learn more, look at taking a course like English for Journalists, an online interactive course provided by NUJ Scotland, www.nujscotland.com.

Common errors and pitfalls

Here are some more areas to watch out for: you may not fall into all these traps but it is worth knowing about them if you are writing for a living.

Singular and plurals
Verbs need to agree with their subject, and sometimes it can be confusing, especially if you are looking at numbers or groups of people.

One in seven people has . . .

A business is singular, even if it appears to have a plural name. *'Marks and Spencer is one of the biggest stores on the high street'*, rather than *'Marks and Spencer are . . .'*

Mixed-up words
It can be easy to mix up the noun 'practice' and the verb 'practise'. If you are unsure, think about 'advice' and 'advise': as they are pronounced differently it can help you remember that 'advice' and 'practice' are the nouns.

One of the most common muddles is 'effect' and 'affect'. Remember that 'affect' is more 'active' i.e. it is the verb.

I affected the outcome.

What was the effect?

'Complimentary' and 'complementary' are two adjectives with different meanings but only one letter difference. 'Complimentary' can mean 'flattering' or 'free'.

She made a complimentary remark about my new book.

The publisher sent out complimentary copies to reviewers.

'Complementary' means 'balancing' or 'completing'.

The complementary volume will be available soon.

Make your own list of words that can be muddled up easily: look at the different meanings when you write:

· disinterested or uninterested;

· imply or infer;
· on a regular basis or regularly;
· biennial or biannual.

American English

For a writer, American English can differ in spelling, punctuation, grammar and vocabulary. Know and understand the difference, and be clear which audience you are writing for. If using a programme like MS Word which has the option to select UK or US English, make sure you select the right option at the start or all your manoeuvres can end up being automatically corrected to maneuvers.

Writing style

When you are writing, your first aim should be clarity. Use short sentences instead of long ones. Check your writing to see if you are using the passive voice:

The book about the history of fashion was written by Alison Smith.

The active voice is easier to understand:

Alison Smith wrote a book about the history of fashion.

Know your own weaknesses

The more you write, the more aware you will become of your own style. I know that I tend to overuse the word 'however', and will scan through an initial draft of whatever I am writing and pull out most occurrences of this word, which often adds very little. One of the most common errors editor Emma Cooper sees is 'Repetition of the same phrase again and again. We all have our favourite phrases, but try not to overuse them.'

Emma has listed more of the most frequent errors that she sees in documents:

· incorrectly spelt foreign words, when listing ingredients or citing the name of a piece of music, a composer, etc.;
· inconsistencies in the use of initial capitals in headings;
· inconsistent use of hyphens in compound words, e.g. online or on-line. If you're not sure, check in the dictionary, but there are

often no hard and fast rules here, so the most important thing is to be consistent within your document.

See it right

One further factor to take into account when writing for commercial clients is the accessibility of the final version of your text. The Disability Discrimination Act gives businesses a legal duty to provide information for blind and partially sighted customers. Something as simple as producing information in a plain typeface in 14 point instead of 10 point can significantly increase the number of people who can read it. This will benefit anyone who might otherwise have to reach for their reading glasses as well as partially sighted people. A good knowledge of how to increase the number of people who can read the copy you produce can be a valuable extra service to sell to your clients.

See www.rnib.org.uk for more information on RNIB's 'See it Right' campaign and their clear print guidelines.

Useful contacts

British Association of Communicators in Business
Suite GA2,
Oak House,
Woodlands Business Park,
Linford Wood,
Milton Keynes MK14 6EY
Tel: 01908 313755
www.cib.uk.com

Chartered Institute of Public Relations
CIPR Public Relations Centre
32 St James's Square
London SW1Y 4JR
Tel: 020 7766 3333
Email: info@cipr.co.uk
www.cipr.co.uk

The Commonwealth Club
25 Northumberland Avenue
London WC2N 5AP
Tel: 020 7766 9200
www.thecommonwealthclub.co.uk

Design and Art Directors' Association (D&AD)
9 Graphite Square
Vauxhall Walk
London SE11 5EE
Tel: 020 7840 1111
www.dandad.org

Institute of Practitioners in Advertising
44 Belgrave Square
London SW1X 8QS
Tel: 020 7235 7020
E-mail: info@ipa.co.uk
www.ipa.co.uk

The London Press Club
St Bride Institute
14 Bride Lane
Fleet Street
London EC4Y 8EQ
Tel: 020 7353 7086/7
www.londonpressclub.co.uk

NABS London (National Advertising Benevolent Society)
47–50 Margaret Street
London W1W 8SB
Email: nabs@nabs.org.uk
Tel: 020 7462 3150
NABS helpline: 0845 602 4497

The National Council for the Training of Journalists
NCTJ Training Ltd
The New Granary
Station Road
Newport
Saffron Walden
Essex CB11 3PL
Tel: 01799 544014
Email: info@nctj.com
www.nctj.com

The National Union of Journalists
Head Office
Headland House
308–12 Gray's Inn Road
London WC1X 8DP
Tel: 020 7278 7916
Email: info@nuj.org.uk
www.nuj.org.uk

The New Cavendish Club
44 Great Cumberland Place
London W1H 8BS
Tel: 020 7723 0391/6
Email: info@newcavendishclub.co.uk

Society for Editors and Proofreaders
Erico House
93–9 Upper Richmond Road
Putney
London SW15 2TG
Tel: 020 8785 5617
Email: administration@sfep.org.uk
www.sfep.org.uk

The Society of Authors
84 Drayton Gardens
London SW10 9SB
Tel: 020 7373 6642
www.societyofauthors.org